WILFRED THESIGER was born in 1910 at the British Legation in Addis Ababa, and spent his early years in Abyssinia. He was educated at Eton and Oxford. In the War, serving with patriots under Orde Wingate in Abyssinia, he was awarded a DSO. He later served with the SOE (in Syria) and the SAS in the Western Desert.

Thesiger's journeys have won him the Founder's Medal of the Royal Geographical Society, the Lawrence of Arabia Medal of the Royal Central Asian Society, the Livingstone Medal of the Royal Scottish Geographical Society and the Burton Memorial Medal of the Royal Asiatic Society.

His writing has won him the Heinemann Award; Fellowship of the Royal Society of Literature; an Honorary D. Litt. from Leicester University and an Honorary D. Litt. from the University of Bath.

In 1968 he was made CBE. He is Honorary Fellow of the British Academy and Honorary Fellow of Magdalen College, Oxford. He was honoured with a KBE in 1995.

For over twenty years, until 1994, he lived mostly among the pastoral Samburu at Maralal in northern Kenya. He now lives permanently in London.

AMONG THE MOUNTAINS

TRAVELS THROUGH ASIA

WILFRED THESIGER

Flamingo
An Imprint of HarperCollins*Publishers*

Flamingo
An Imprint of HarperCollins*Publishers*
77–85 Fulham Palace Road,
Hammersmith, London W6 8JB

www.**fire**and**water**.com

Published by Flamingo 2000
1 3 7 5 7 9 6 4 2

First published in Great Britain by
HarperCollins*Publishers* 1998

Author photograph © Johnny Haddock

ISBN 0 00 655100 9

Set in Linotype Minion

Printed and bound in Great Britain by Clays Ltd, St Ives plc

In memory of my Father
my lifelong inspiration

CONTENTS

LIST OF MAPS

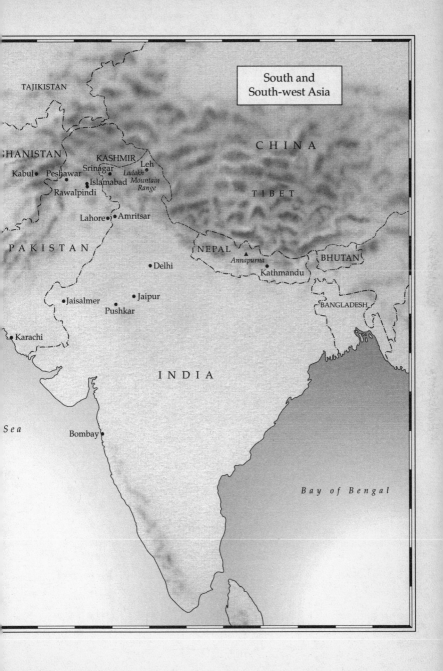

South and
South-west Asia

TAJIKISTAN

CHINA

AFGHANISTAN

KASHMIR

Kabul Peshawar Srinagar Leh

Islamabad *Ladakh Mountain Range*

Rawalpindi

TIBET

Lahore Amritsar

PAKISTAN

NEPAL

Annapurna

BHUTAN

Delhi

Kathmandu

Jaisalmer Jaipur

Pushkar

BANGLADESH

Karachi

INDIA

Sea

Bombay

Bay of Bengal

GLOSSARY

ailoq (Persian): herdsmen's summer pasture camp

arbob: a hereditary district chief or headman

chenar: a variety of plane tree

dak (Hindustani): as in dak bungalow, a rest-house for travellers

ghee (Hindustani): clarified butter

havildar (Persian): Sepoy officer rank corresponding to sergeant

ibex (Latin): a species of wild mountain goat with large recurved horns found in Europe, North Africa and Central Asia

Imra: the benign god Creator, a principal deity in the Kafir pantheon

jemadar (Anglo-Indian colloq. Urdu): a junior native officer in the Indian army

kizilbash: a headman

lammergeyer (German): large bearded vulture with six-foot wingspan

markhor (Pushtu): a species of wild mountain goat with large spiralled horns, found in northern India and Tibet

malik (Arabic): a village headman, owner or employer (in Arabia, a king)

mudhif (Arabic): a Sheik's barrel-vaulted, reed-built guest-house in and around the Marshes of southern Iraq

mullah (Arabic): variously an Islamic teacher, priest or leader

munshi: a teacher, usually of language

névés pénitents (French): a rare formation of snow and ice pinnacles bearing some resemblance to cowled monks

Ovis poli (Latin): a species of Asiatic wild sheep with large, wide-spreading horns named after the Venetian traveller, Marco Polo

rabab: a stringed, musical instrument resembling a viol

sayid (Arabic): a person having or claiming descent from the Prophet

seer (Hindustani): Indian measure of weight (varying) approximately equivalent to 2 pounds

serai (Persian): as in caravanserai, an Eastern quadrangular inn with a great inner court where caravans put up

shai khana: a tea-house

shikari (Anglo-Indian/Hindustani): a hunter

sitar (Hindustani): a long-necked, stringed, Indian musical instrument resembling a lute

tonga (Hindustani): a light two-wheeled vehicle used in rural areas of India

urial (Punjabi): a species of Himalayan wild sheep

Wali (Arabic/Turkish): a local civil Governor, e.g. the Wali of Swat

wazir (Arabic): minister or councillor of state

yurt (Turkish): a Turkoman nomad's felt tent

ACKNOWLEDGEMENTS

MY ORIGINAL INTENTION had been to produce a book of the photographs I took in the Karakorams and the Hindu Kush between 1952 and 1965. I have never kept a diary with a view to publication. Indeed I had never looked again at the diaries of my mountain journeys, except to refer to them briefly when I wrote *Desert, Marsh and Mountain* almost twenty years ago. Now I only thought of using them to help me write the captions for my photographs.

My biographer and very close friend, Alexander Maitland, had, however, read these diaries, and he assured me that they contained more than enough material for a full-length text. This is what I then decided to do and Alex as always gave me every assistance. Without his help this book could never have been written. I am also grateful for the help and encouragement of my editors, Lucinda McNeile and Emma Harrison-Topham; and to Philip Lewis who helped me to select the photographs and designed the layout.

In 1993 I sent my collection of photographs to the Pitt-Rivers Museum in Oxford. I am grateful to the Museum's Assistant Curator, Dr Elizabeth Edwards, who transferred all the photograph albums I required to my flat in London.

I wish to thank the Royal Geographical Society for permission to quote from articles published in the *Geographical*

Journal Vol. CXXI, Part 3, September 1955, and Vol. CXXIII, Part 4, December 1957, describing my journeys in the Hazarajat and Nuristan. The present text also includes brief extracts reprinted from my previous books, *Desert, Marsh and Mountain* and *Visions of a Nomad*.

Looking back, I now wish that I had kept a more detailed record of my second journey in Nuristan, in 1965, and my travels in Ladakh. Otherwise, the months devoted to preparing this book have brought me constant pleasure. Reading my diaries again has revived memories of companionships which meant much to me, in areas whose ways of life have now changed for ever.

Wilfred Thesiger
London, 1997

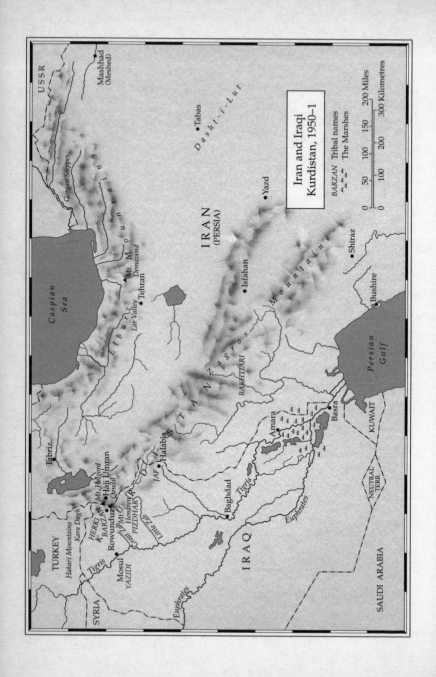

Iran and Iraqi
Kurdistan, 1950–1

BARZAN Tribal names
🌾🌾 The Marshes

0   50   100 150 200 Miles
0   100 200   300 Kilometres

PREFACE
IRAQI KURDISTAN
1950–1

MOUNTAINS HAVE ALWAYS attracted me, and when I am among them I have wished to see as much of them as possible. I am, however, without training or technical skill as a mountaineer. Indeed only once, in the High Atlas in Morocco, have I been on a rope. Compared with the challenges offered by the desert, or country inhabited by hostile tribes such as the Danakil in Ethiopia, I sense no personal challenge in an unclimbed mountain face. On the contrary, I would always seek to find the easiest way over or round a mountain, in order to see what lay beyond. I always preferred to travel on my own and would never have wished to join an organized mountaineering expedition. Instead I travelled with a few locals, believing that if they could cross a high pass I would be able to do the same. Admittedly, they could sleep, wrapped in cloaks, under a rock, whereas I needed a bivvy tent.

I had always dreamt of travelling one day in the Himalayas, the Karakorams or the Hindu Kush and I had been fascinated when, in 1944, I read Eric Shipton's book *Upon That Mountain*. I was captivated by Shipton's personality and empathized strongly with his concept of mountaineering. Though an outstanding mountaineer, Shipton seemed to me essentially an explorer, more eager to discover what lay behind a range of mountains than to climb a still unconquered mountain face. In

1949, on my way back to England from Oman, I travelled briefly through Persia by car, from Bushire to Shiraz, Isfahan, Tehran and Tabriz, then on through Kurdistan to Baghdad. As we climbed over the pass at Haji Umran, into Iraq, I felt an uplift of the spirit. The mountains, some of them snow-capped, looked magnificent. I felt, at once, an urge to return and travel through them.

Never had I seen such country: the great rock-girt bastion of Hendren above the gorge of Rowunduz; Helgord's twelve thousand feet; the snow-capped range of Qandil, with sheer-faced precipices of five thousand feet; and, higher still, beyond the Turkish frontier, Kara Dagh, the 'Black Mountain'. Everywhere one range was superimposed upon another. The knees of the mountains and the valley sides up to six thousand feet were wooded with holly-oaks interspersed with ash, hawthorn and wild pear, and rare stands of juniper. In the valley bottoms the Zab, the Little Zab and other smaller rivers and torrents flowed down to join the far-off Tigris, foaming ice-cold through narrow gorges of polished rock and swirling among great boulders fallen from the cliffs above; or calm in deep green pools under grassy banks and overhanging willows.

I returned to Iraqi Kurdistan for three months in August 1950 and for another five months the following May. I suspect that few foreigners had ever seen as much of this country as I did during those eight months; there can have been few villages I did not visit, few mountains I did not climb. Without the urge to hunt I should never have seen half the country that I did, nor looked on many a stupendous view. I was accompanied by a cheerful, good-natured and indefatigable young Kurd called Nasser, who spoke Arabic. I knew no Kurdish and only a few of the chiefs, or aghas, spoke Arabic. Sometimes we hired a mule or a horse to carry our saddle-bags, while we walked; at other times our hosts lent us horses to our next destination, and then we rode. As usual I took little with me: some spare clothes and a couple of blankets in case we camped out, a few medicines, a book or two – *Lord Jim* and *Kim* have been stand-bys on many of my journeys – a camera, and my Rigby .275 rifle. On subsequent journeys among the mountains of Pakistan, Afghanistan and Nuristan I did not take a rifle. I did then have a small tent, but otherwise my kit remained the same.

In Kurdistan we relied on our hosts for food and bedding. More welcoming and hospitable than Persian villagers, they would have felt insulted if we had fed ourselves. Mostly we ate flaps of unleavened bread with curds, or boiled wheat, sometimes meat and vegetable stews with rice. In season there was fruit: mulberries, apricots, peaches, melons; sometimes I gorged on grapes, freshly picked and warmed by the sun or cooled in a nearby stream.

In spring there were the wild flowers: red or white anemones on the lower slopes, covering whole hillsides with carpets of colour; and among them red ranunculus, yellow marigolds, gladioli, stocks, dark blue squills and irises. High up on the mountains scarlet tulips grew in profusion, scattered tiger lilies flowered in hollows among the rocks, dark blue gentians bordered drifts of snow.

In such a setting the Kurds in tasselled turbans were fittingly colourful. The Jaf, who lived in the south round Halabja and had been nomadic till Persia closed the frontier, wore long robes like the Arabs, with short jackets over elaborately wound cummerbunds and baggy trousers drawn in at the ankle. The northern Kurds, the nomadic Herki in particular, wore loose, wide-bottomed trousers and tucked their jackets under their cummerbunds. Whereas the Jaf wore dark uniform colours, the clothes of the northern tribes were dyed in blues, greens and browns of varying shades, woven with wide, light-coloured stripes and patterns. Most men were hung about with bandoliers, all wore formidable daggers in their cummerbunds and often carried revolvers in holsters at their sides.

The most interesting character I met in Kurdistan was Sheikh Mahmud. Intensely ambitious and aspiring to rule an independent Kurdistan, he had led his tribesmen in insurrection after insurrection from 1919 to 1930 against the British who then controlled Iraq. Defeated each time after fierce fighting, he would be exiled, pardoned and allowed to return, only to rebel once more. His last uprising was against the Iraqis in 1941. I had known him well by repute. A stout, jovial figure, Sheikh Mahmud often entertained me in his house: in the evening, after we had fed, he would recall ancient battles and British officers he had known. A few years later he died. I am glad I met him.

Nasser and I stayed in villages of flat-roofed houses rising in tiers up the hillsides and slept in rooms furnished only with rugs and pillows; we shared the black tents, or cabins built from branches in which the tribes lived after they had moved in spring with their herds to the mountainsides. I remember coming down from Helgord, tired and thirsty, to the tents of the Baliki pitched on green turf where yellow buttercups and pink primulas flowered among the moss, bordering threads of water and shallow pools. How good the yoghurt they gave me tasted.

In Kurdistan I climbed innumerable mountain faces looking for bear and ibex. On one occasion I slipped crossing a tongue of frozen snow and slid for thirty yards or more down the icy slope towards a precipice. Luckily, the gradient eased and I clawed to a stop. After that I always wore felt-soled Kurdish slippers, the best footwear on such mountains. But in all my months in Kurdistan I only shot one bear and one ibex.

On several of those hunts I was accompanied by a tireless Assyrian, named Raihana, a former officer of the Iraq Levies. He was well informed about the wildlife of the mountains. During our hunts we sometimes camped in the woods or slept in caves. One night we were woken by the 'woof' of a bear which found us in possession of its home under a rock by a small pool. Bears were not uncommon, especially in the north, but I saw only four. Sometimes we spotted ibex, threading their way across the face of a sheer precipice without apparent footholds – we would sit and watch them while griffon vultures circled above us or a lammergeyer sailed past on motionless wings, so close that I could see the bristles that gave it its other name, the bearded vulture; and always there were choughs, swooping and tumbling shrill-voiced around the crags. Not infrequently we disturbed wild boar in the woods, and once I saw a roe deer. Wolves were fairly common and took a toll from the flocks, and in the remoter areas there were said to be some leopard.

With Nasser, I travelled for some four hundred miles throughout the length and breadth of Iraqi Kurdistan, passing more than once through the territories of the Baradost, Mungur, Pizdhar, Jaf and other tribes. Then, far to the south, we left the mountains and reached the plains where Kurd merged into Arab.

Here we found ourselves among the Bani Lam, one of the great shepherd tribes of southern Iraq. Escorted by our hosts and riding on their horses, we travelled from one encampment to the next until we came at last to the town of Amara. Beyond Amara lay the strange remote world of the Iraqi Marshes where I was to live for seven years.

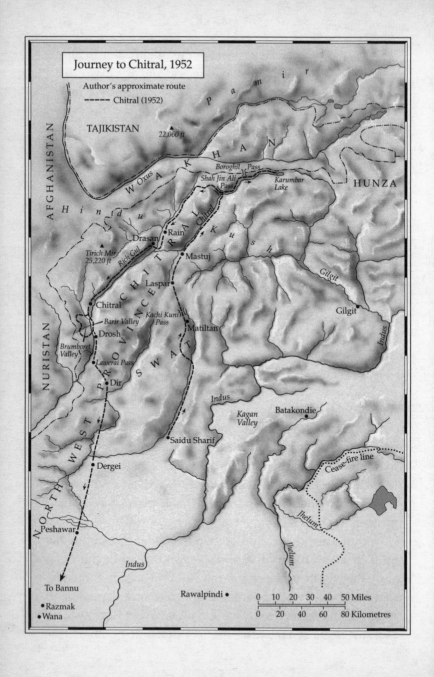

Journey to Chitral, 1952

Author's approximate route
----- Chitral (1952)

TAJIKISTAN

22,060 ft

AFGHANISTAN

Hindu

Pamir

W A K H A N

R Oxus

Boroghil Pass
Shah Jin Ali Pass

Karumbar Lake

HUNZA

Tirich Mir 25,220 ft

Drasan   Rain

Rich Gul

CHITRAL

Chitral Kunar

Mastuj

Gilgit

Laspar

NURISTAN

Chitral
Barir Valley
Drosh

Brumboret Valley

Lawerai Pass

Dir

Kachi Kuni Pass

Matiltan

PROVINCE

Gilgit

Indus

SWAT

Indus

Kagan Valley

Batakondie

Saidu Sharif

NORTH WEST

Dergei

Cease-fire line

Peshawar

Jhelum

To Bannu

• Razmak
• Wana

Rawalpindi •

Indus

Jhelum

0   10 20 30 40 50 Miles
0   20   40   60   80 Kilometres

CHITRAL

1952

ARLY IN 1952, during a brief visit to London, I invited Eric
Shipton to lunch with me at the Travellers' Club when he
suggested I travel in Hunza in northern Pakistan. He told me
that the sight of Rakaposhi from Baltit was one of the finest
sights he had seen. I returned to the Marshes in February, having already planned to spend the following autumn travelling
in the mountains of northern Pakistan.

I left the Marshes in July 1952 and flew from Basra to
Karachi.

At Rawalpindi, in northern Pakistan, I tried unsuccessfully to
obtain from an official who proved evasive permission to
travel through Chitral and back through Hunza. In the end, I
took the letter of introduction I had with me from Sir George
Cunningham, a former Governor of the North-West Frontier
Province, to the Governor, Khwaja Shahabud Din, in Peshawar. When I left his house, I had his permission to travel
wherever I wished in the states of Swat and Chitral, but
unfortunately not in Hunza which lay outside his province.

In Peshawar I engaged a bearer called Jahangir Khan, who
spoke some English, and a few days later, on 22 August, I left
Peshawar by bus for Saidu Sharif in Swat. On the way there we
stayed a night at Malakand where I dined in the mess of a

Punjabi battalion and slept in the dak bungalow, or rest-house. Next morning the Chief Secretary of Swat took me with him to Saidu Sharif where I called on the ruler, the Wali of Swat. He authorized me to cross the Kachi Kuni Pass into Chitral; but he did warn me that the 16,000-foot pass was difficult and said that, as far as he knew, it had never been crossed by any European. I doubted this, but I did feel daunted when I first saw the mountains, for which my equipment, a bivvy tent, rucksack, some solid fuel and an ice axe, seemed rather inadequate.

On 26 August with Jahangir Khan I drove in the Wali's bus to Baraini, and from there we set off on foot along a well-made path with two mules, a muleteer and an armed man as escort. At first, the narrow valley and thick clouds covering the mountains restricted the view. The mountainsides were steep, covered with holly-oak and deodars; the river here was milky-coloured and fast-flowing. Some walnut trees grew near the occasional villages where there was maize growing on small terraces; we bought plums, apples and a few grapes.

At intervals we passed successions of drab-coloured villagers, a few with mules or donkeys but most of them carrying loads.

We spent the night at Kulali, in a primitive caravanserai immediately below the Chodgram fort. Next day, after walking for five hours through more deodar forest, by mid-afternoon we reached Kalam village, a most impressive spot at an altitude of 6,500 feet, situated in a basin enclosed by high, very steep mountains. Until we arrived at Kalam, where the villagers were cutting their hay, we had seen few houses and little cultivation. From here we had a fine view of a mountain covered with snow, further up the Ushu Valley. In the evening, some of the villagers played a Chitrali mandolin accompanied by a drum. The tunes sounded almost like ours.

I hung about in Kalam in the morning in the hopes of getting some photographs, but the weather remained overcast. Eventually we left and made our way up the valley of the Ushu through forests of pine and deodar. At Ushu there was a fort built on a rise, overlooking the village, and some large graveyards. The graves were roofed over with wooden planks, most of which had ultimately fallen in, so that they appeared like cavities in the ground. Some of the better constructed ones were shaped like boats and their wooden sides were often embellished with carvings. Elaborately carved posts also marked the head and foot of the graves. Many of them were decorated with the horns of ibex and markhor. At the graves of holy men, passers-by would stop and say a prayer.

Most of the day remained overcast, cold and rather cheerless, with rain in the afternoon. We spent the rest of the day at Matiltan, where we put up in a small dark room opposite the entrance to the fort. The locals, an unwashed crowd, smelt overpowering when huddled together indoors. The fort, commanded by a jemadar, was manned by the Wali's retainers armed with antiquated rifles. I now needed four or five porters, to replace the mules I had brought with me from Baraini, and there were arguments about their pay. The men told me they wanted twenty rupees each to take me over the pass. At Matiltan there was only one shop and nothing to be had except a few very expensive chickens and eggs.

Next morning, more arguments about the porters' wages delayed us but we had finally compromised at fifteen rupees as far as Laspur and they agreed to provide their own food. Four men would carry the loads, which I had thought would require five, for what would probably be five days' journey; two of the Wali's retainers from the fort were ordered to accompany us.

We eventually reached Mahodand just as it was getting dark, after coming up the valley by an easy track through woods of fir, pine and deodar. The mountains rose up very sheer on both sides of the valley, above a fast-flowing stretch of the river. On the way, we passed Paloga where a shrine consisted of a log cabin decorated with horns of ibex and markhor. Less than an hour after leaving Paloga, we stopped at Ishgal, a hamlet with half a dozen or so houses, each house with some terraced maize round it, and Jahangir and I ate our lunch of eggs and chapattis. From Ishgal, the forests rose more than 400 to 500 feet up the mountains on either side of the valley. After a steep climb through a dark wood, where the fir trees grew close together, we came out on to an open meadow about a mile across and two miles long with green grass, flowers and a small pool. The river, here coloured milky blue, flowed through it without a ripple.

At Mahodand we heard that wolves were numerous and the river was said to be full of trout which the villagers caught with a hook and line. On the way there we had passed several woodland shrines consisting of heaped-up branches and logs; in the pine wood below Mahodand there were any number of large, single stones or else small stones piled on the rocks which, as far as I could make out, marked the site of a battle. I saw hardly any flowers, apart from those in the meadow near Mahodand, and very few birds except for one snipe and a hoopoe.

At Mahodand there were two lots of houses. I noticed a fair number of cows, some goats, small sturdy ponies and donkeys. There were few dogs. When I tried to buy a chicken for dinner, I was asked for two rupees for a very small one and so, instead, I bought quite a large goat for fifteen rupees. We killed the goat by moonlight and with the help of pine flares cut it up. We divided the meat between ourselves and the porters, and the man we had bought it from helped to eat it. We made some good, if rather goaty, soup.

The porters came along very well all day and averaged three miles per hour. Every mile they had a short rest. They carried the loads, which probably weighed 50–60 pounds, on their backs with ropes under each arm. They wrapped their feet up in sacking covered with goat skin which they bound round their feet with a leather thong, leaving the big toe outside. They then wrapped the sacking round their calves like puttees, but very bulky ones, bound all the way round with the thong. Everyone here wore the Chitrali cap; shirt, trousers and a blanket over all.

The next day I wandered round getting some photographs of the valley and its inhabitants, who liked being photographed. We set off at about eight and went slowly up the valley, crossing a succession of grassy meadows interspersed with small fir woods. There were rapids in the river. Now and then in these fir woods we passed houses built from large logs slotted to fit into each other and roofed with more logs and branches. The houses were square-shaped and some of them had stone walls. We met a party going down to Mahodand on horseback.

Shortly before eleven, we stopped on the tree-line near some houses. The mountainsides were now quite bare and there were jagged peaks at the end of the valley. Looking back the way we had come, I could see the snow-covered mountains above Matiltan.

We were now above the fir woods. Every now and again we passed through birch woods growing along the water's edge. The birch bark was like paper and I was told that the locals used it as a wrapping material. From here we climbed steadily to Loe Pan Ghala, where we spent the night. We passed some encampments, including one where they were shearing their sheep. There were more goats about than sheep.

Loe Pan Ghala consisted of four or five huts, roofed with tree trunks and branches supported on wooden uprights, built under some overhanging rocks. The largest house was quite comfortable and accommodated all of us. It was a still night and we were able to have an unsheltered candle.

The journey from Loe Pan Ghala over the Kachi Kuni Pass to Laspur took more than two days. The first day involved a series of pretty steep climbs, broken by easy going over occasional grassy flats. Near Loe Pan Ghala the hillsides were covered with a small red flower like sorrel. From a distance this gave an effect like heather. Otherwise, flowers were scarce, and then mostly daisies. Further on, the mountainsides were bare rock, with much scree where there had been landslides. The peaks all round us had snow on them and seemed quite close. Here the river was little more than a stream. We rested at midday and cooked a meal over a fire of dry bog myrtle, then carried on over more rocky debris where the going was rough and the cracked, crumbling earth looked as if it would not take much to start another landslide.

By late afternoon we were climbing the mountain itself by a steep scrambling route which, in places, led over small glaciers. Away to our right I saw an ice-fall, at the end of a small glacier, at the head of the valley we had just come up. While it was still light, we pitched the tent on a narrow ledge and cooked our dinner using the solid fuel and water from a stream we found trickling beneath some boulders. The porters made themselves shelters under the rocks.

During the night three or four inches of snow fell and everything was white when I came out of the tent at sunrise. This was very Christmas-like but inopportune. The porters seemed remarkably cheerful despite their night in the open at about 13,000 feet without anything but a blanket apiece. I was afraid they would refuse to go on, but they started without a murmur and without breakfast.

The sky all round looked stormy, the clouds lit red by the rising sun. There were occasional flurries of light snow. We climbed steadily for three hours until we reached the 16,000-foot summit of the Kachi Kuni Pass. For about half the climb we found frozen snow overlaid by last night's fall. I went ahead and cut steps. The rest of the climb was over jumbled boulders also hidden by the fresh snow. I was glad to find that I did not feel the least tired or breathless, except that my arms got tired from step cutting. Several of the porters complained of headaches.

When we got to the top there were fitful glimpses of the sun, but the distant mountains were smothered in cloud. We could see the tarn where we lunched the day before, far below us at the bottom of a black, shadow-filled gorge.

After a brief halt we started off again, over a smooth, snow-covered glacier. One of the porters, who knew the glacier, went ahead with me roped to him. It sloped gradually downhill, but the last hour involved a fairly steep descent to the bottom past an impressive ice-fall on our left.

We continued on following the stream down the valley, which fell quite steeply. We camped eventually under a large, overhanging rock with a few birch trees nearby. Apart from these trees the landscape was very bleak, and the mountain-sides to our right and left merely bare rock and earth.

A fine snow-covered mountain dominated the valley behind us. Coming down the glacier we had passed below this mountain, but it had been too close for us to get a proper view.

The following day, after walking for about four hours in bright sunshine down the bare, boulder-strewn valley, we arrived at Laspur, a small village attractively situated beside the stream, bordered here by some very green turf, poplars and fields of wheat. The dak bungalow where we stayed had been used to stable the villagers' animals. Some of the cows I saw had been crossed with yaks.

Several boys carried bows, about two feet long with a double string held apart at one end by a short stick; the strings were joined in the middle by a small leather pouch and the bow was used, like a catapult, to shoot stones. In Chitral, almost all the men and boys carried these bows.

The four porters left to go back to Matiltan and Jahangir Khan and I went on to Mastuj, carrying our kit on two donkeys. I found this a slow and wearisome way of travelling. At one village the women wore skull caps and looked, to me, far more Mongolian in appearance than the men, with their hair in two plaits down each side of their faces. Small herd boys ran about naked in the hot sun.

Mastuj, like all the Chitrali villages, I was told, consisted of a number of scattered farmsteads. The houses were built from stones and mud, each with an orchard inside the stone wall surrounding it. There were poplars, willows, fruit trees and some hemp; and fields of corn, most of which had already been cut. Wild roses grew along the lanes. There was a fine view down the valley of Tirich Mir. This snow-covered mountain with its graceful peak was the highest in the Hindu Kush; its 25,200-foot summit towered over other snowy mountains of 20,000 feet. The mountainsides were very steep, with evidence of many landslides, and the mountain opposite Mastuj had its lower slopes eroded into curious formations.

*

I spent the next two days at Mastuj, where I met Major Mohiuddin of the Guides Cavalry, a friendly, helpful young man of about twenty-six, and his elder brother, Lieutenant-Colonel Khushwaqt-al-Mulk, of the 3rd Royal Frontier Force Rifles, uncles of the ruler of Chitral. The first evening, after dinner, the major laid on a dance. The band consisted of a bass drum, kettledrums, a tambourine, flutes and pipes which sounded rather like bagpipes. A single person danced at a time, each dance different from the one before.

The following afternoon I was invited to play polo. I had never played the game before but the major and his brother insisted that it was time I learnt. The previous night a pipe band had played to announce the match, and now the same band played at intervals during the game and again after it finished. The polo field, 600 yards long by about 70 yards wide, had a stone wall on either side, a shallow ditch in the middle and rocks to mark the goals. There were no rules. We played five a side and the two chukkers were of indeterminate length. I probably hit the ball only half-a-dozen times but it was great fun. It was in these parts, and in such games as this, that polo originated.

The major had instructed a man called Malung, and his sixteen-year-old son, to take me from Mastuj to the Karumbar lake where the Chitral river rises. We bought more food in the small market and, after loading Malung's horse and a donkey which he produced, we set off early. I remember seeing wild roses in bloom along the track near a settlement where, many years earlier, the farms had been wiped out by a terrific landslide. Further up the valley, we carried our kit across a loop of the river and then drove the horse and donkey high over a shoulder of the mountain. This wasted a lot of time.

At Brep, where we spent the night in a small rest-house, nearly all the inhabitants had goitre.

From here on we stopped every evening at a farmstead. The flat-roofed houses looked unprepossessing from the outside, but inside revealed a soundly constructed framework of massive, well-fashioned posts and beams. Directly above an open hearth, the roof was built up to a funnel-shaped opening which let out the smoke. Men and boys hereabouts wore the circular Chitrali cap with its distinctive, wide tubular rim and overcoats of oatmeal-coloured homespun. The women all went unveiled.

To reach the next village, we had to climb between 2,000 and 2,500 feet up the shoulder of a mountain overhanging the river. There was lightning and thunder on the mountaintops across the river. A sharp shower of rain fell just as we got to the village where we lunched, sheltering in a small dark room. By the time we stopped for the night at Wasam it was already dark and Jahangir Khan was pretty weary. We stayed in a house owned by a refugee from Afghanistan, whose wife remained in the room with us and poured out the tea.

Swathes of smoky cloud had hidden the mountains from view the previous day and they were still wreathed in cloud when we left early in the morning. As far as I could see the mountains appeared very jagged and steep. There were birch coppices with small streams oozing through them in the valley as far as Dobargar, and quite a lot of juniper, stunted trees between six and eight feet high.

Opposite Nakiadam were some spectacular mountains: snow-covered peaks broken by rocks and precipices and, lower down, long stretches of pale-grey scree only a shade darker than the snow. The mountains here varied in colour from purple-black to red, brick-brown and from almost salmon-pink to ivory. They looked like the sort of mountains where you might expect to find wild sheep, quite different from the precipitous ibex mountains we had seen so far. These mountains were in Yarkhun, the most attractive mountains I had seen so far on this journey.

The afternoon stayed grey and overcast, with a cold west wind and Scotch mist. We arrived at Lasht after dark in heavy rain. We had to climb over a steep hill before getting to the river crossing, a crude pole bridge below the village, and then had to unload the animals to get them across the bridge. From there we stumbled through the dark and rain until we came to a small house where we took refuge. In places the going had been fairly hard. Some of the time we had to climb up to get round sheer cliffs of sedimentary deposit. Malung seemed a bit downhearted after his two long days trekking and Jahangir Khan sighed audibly for the cantonments at Peshawar.

On 9 September we set off in grey, raw morning weather with the mountains shrouded in mist. We passed some cultivated fields and then through woods of poplar, willow and thorn where I noticed the first autumn tints; then out on to a hillside covered with more stunted juniper, a strangely old-looking tree like yew. Coming round the slope of Gharqab we had to unload the horse and donkey and carry the loads along a steep face of scree where there was almost no track. The sun had come out by then but the mountains were still largely hidden in mist and haze.

Generally speaking there were few birds to be seen: an occasional magpie, a few doves, black and white chats and choughs among the cliffs. Where a stream from the west shoulder of

Gharqab joined the river, I saw a mallard, two falcons and an eagle with dark plumage and a white-banded tail.

In the afternoon we stopped at a house whose owner insisted on our spending the night, saying it was going to rain and the next village was a long way off. Towards sunset it indeed began to rain and turned cold. The house had a big central room on two levels where the fire was and the family lived and cooked. Off this was a smaller room where we slept. The owner's twelve-year-old daughter had diarrhoea and pains in her stomach; I gave her some Chloromycetin. During the evening three Afghans arrived, wearing turbans and high boots. I gathered that these men were refugees.

Until the sun was properly up the next day felt bitterly cold. The people themselves, I noticed, wrapped up warmly, but many of the boys and small children went barefoot. A young boy with pronounced Tartar features came with us as far as Wadinkot. Here we found one of the previous night's Afghans and a Kirghiz, very Mongolian in appearance, with a thin straggling beard. I photographed both of them. The villagers gave us some good bread and curds.

I had some magnificent views of the 22,000-foot snow mountains across a glacier further up the valley from Wadinkot. We stopped for the night at a two-roomed house near a bridge, where a munshi with an irregular guard of eight armed men lived for ten months a year. We had passed some stone-built houses inhabited by Wakikh from Warkhand who are now refugees on this side of the border. Some Kazakh also lived in these parts, but mostly Wakikh.

We left at 7 AM accompanied by the munshi Sharwal Jafar Mamad, who rode a horse and carried a Lee-Enfield rifle. We crossed the river by the pole-and-brushwood bridge near the munshi's house and carried on along the bank past small fields of wheat which had just been cut but not gathered, and some stone houses belonging to the Wakikh.

From here we had a fine view of the snowy peaks and also of the Chiantu glacier. The mountains round us were not very high though they had some snow on them; those across the river were higher. We passed no more dwellings until we reached Shuasir. The surrounding country was very bare and here the river divided in small channels, flowing through an expanse of sand and pebbles. The water was a curious chalky colour with sediment in it. We found some yaks at Shuasir, the first I had ever seen; they were mostly black, but one was pure white and several others parti-coloured. At sunset a few men turned up riding on yaks, which they guided by a rope fastened to the yak's nose. A Sarakouli, whom I photographed, wore a curious hat shaped rather like an admiral's.

The next morning, I left the others behind and went on ahead with the Sharwal up the valley to Karumbar; he was riding his horse and I was riding Malung's. It was very cold at first light and there were icicles along the edges of the streams. We arrived at Karumbar at 10, left again at 11, and got back to camp at 3 P.M.

The country between Shuasir and Karumbar was most exhilarating, great tawny mountainsides across which cloud shadows drifted and, higher up, the snows and glaciers very white and clear in the thin, cold mountain air. Here was the space and cleanliness of the desert combined with the great heights and the clear blue sky of central Asia.

As far as Zhuil we rode along the side of a rather stony mountain, with small hollows below us in which were pools of very blue water and reddish-golden patches of bog laced with a network of little streams. Beyond this was the wide expanse of the river-bed, grey sand and shingle, and behind this the stony, black, snow-sprinkled foothills of the main snow range, whose higher peaks and glaciers stood up against the sky.

Beyond Zhuil we rode up a wide valley. The stream ran down it through russet-coloured bogs, which also spread up on to the lower slopes of the mountains. The mountains on either side, rocky and snow-covered near their summits, sloped gently down into the valley. The higher rocks were dark in colour, almost a purple-black, but the lower slopes were lighter, banded in shades of pale brick-red, yellow and grey. The lighter coloured rocks were granite.

I saw several coveys of partridges, a few ravens and an occasional hoopoe. Choughs, as usual, were much in evidence and there were quite a lot of kestrels about. Here, too, were many marmots that sat above their burrows and whistled at us as we passed.

The watershed at Karumbar was barely noticeable. The lake, about three miles long, with its deep blue waters, lay on the far side of it. The map gave the lake's altitude at 14,250 feet. The mountains immediately above the lake on its south side were thickly covered with snow and a few patches lay near the lake.

At its west end, by a small stone shelter built under a rock with a cairn on top of it, we found a man with very Mongolian features, well dressed in a mulberry-coloured surcoat, high boots and a fur-lined cap with ear-flaps. With him was a bearded Afghan mullah, and their young servant, a boy in Chitrali clothes. They had two horses with them, one of which had a good Kazakh saddle decorated with silver. They were eating dried bread and drinking a weak, straw-coloured, sugarless tea when we arrived. I said in English, 'Good morning, gentlemen.' It seemed silly to say *Salaam alaikum*, and not to be able to follow it up in Persian, Turki or whatever language they spoke. The Mongol, who later told me he was called Ahmed, smiled and asked us in English to come and join them. While I was drinking tea from one of their small, handleless cups, he asked me if I spoke German. I said, 'Only French and Arabic, I am afraid,' and he replied, 'My friend the mullah speaks Arabic.' Shades of *Kim* and the 'Great Game', I thought. I gathered that they were on their way to Kashgar, where Shipton had been Consul after the Second World War. I would have given much to have travelled with them, but times had changed and the boundaries of our world had closed in. At first Ahmed refused to be photographed but then suddenly agreed.

We left them and rode back to Shuasir. I had bought a sheep that morning for fifteen rupees and had told Jahangir Khan to keep it tied up. But after I left for Karumbar he loosed it and sent it off with the rest of the flock. The result was that we could not get hold of it again until nearly sunset, and Jahangir Khan produced a filthy dinner in the dark, which made me angry.

Sharwal Jafar Mamad and I left at 7 A M the next morning for the Boroghil Pass, both of us riding his horse. There was a strong, very cold wind blowing and I soon found it too cold to ride. We went up over a broken, rocky hillside, past a small, crystal clear lake in a damp hollow, to the pass. From the top of the pass, gazing out over the mountains of Wakhan, I could see in the far distance the glinting waters of the Oxus, which the Sharwal called Ab-i-Panja, flowing through a broad shingle bed at the foot of some dark mountains. We then descended past several small lakes, very clear and in certain lights looking almost indigo-coloured. They were edged with golden-coloured bog and some had reeds growing round their sides.

The views of the snow range south of Boroghil were magnificent. Its higher peaks towered into a cloudless and very blue sky. On the way back we stopped at a house for some dried bread and tea which the locals drank with milk and flavoured with salt. We rested in the hot mid-morning sun, watching some yaks and cows grazing, while the occupants of the house drove their sheep and goats out to pasture. When we got back to the munshi's house in the valley by the bridge, we saw men and women in the fields, trying to keep the pigeons and ubiquitous choughs off their harvest of cut and standing corn.

Early the following morning, we set off from the munshi's house and after two hours arrived back at Wadinkot, where we had stayed the previous week. For the first time I saw a man smoking opium. He heated a small quantity of powdered opium over a flame and then put it into a pipe, using a needle. Further on, at Khankhon, where we stopped for the night at a Sayid's house, a field nearby was full of poppies and hemp. Many houses in this area grew a patch of poppies for opium. The Sayid had dysentery and his brother had died of it ten days before, so I gave him some Chloromycetin.

When we arrived the next day at Yoshkish, high up on the mountainside near Nakiadam, I had a fine view of the snow-white mountains above Khankhon, and a really magnificent prospect of other snow peaks down the valley. Yoshkish occupied an attractive position at the head of some terraced fields. Poplars and willows, all turning to gold, grew round the scattered houses; as elsewhere, the corn had been cut but still not gathered in. All we got to eat here were some unripe apples. Coming from Lasht to Yoshkish we passed a succession of farmsteads and fields, with the Yarkhun mountains always above us. Twice on the way, at the far end of the gorge, I glimpsed the 22,500-foot summit of the range.

We were told that the path over the Shah jin Ali Pass was bad, so the local Hakim came with us, and six men to carry the loads and save our animals.

We left early, climbing steadily and steeply by a fair track, with only one pitch of 300 yards that was really severe along the edge of the stream. I saw a number of petroglyphs, crude rock carvings featuring representations of ibex with large horns; these showed no sign of weathering and stood out very white on the grey rock. We left the main stream and followed a smaller one, veering to the right, after about three miles. Steep cliffs rose up on both sides of the gorge where we came across some juniper and birch.

After about four hours we halted in a grassy depression near the stream and ate lunch, after which I sent the Hakim and his men back to Yoshkish.

We climbed again steadily for an hour, and then crossed some undulating grassland to the watershed. The views all around from the summit of the pass were magnificent. To the south-east, the snow mountains beyond the Yarkhun river; to the north, and very close, jagged granite peaks coloured rose pink and buff. Once I saw an eagle soaring high above us. I guessed the Shah jin Ali Pass to be about 13,000 feet above sea-level; later, looking it up in Schomberg's book, *Kafirs and Glaciers*, I found that he gave its height as 13,975 feet.

Behind the pastel-coloured granite peaks to the north-west lay a great, rounded black mass of mountains with two great snow-caps on their summit. Down the valley of the Rich Gul, the graceful peak of Tirich Mir seemed to tower over everything in its vicinity, even mountains of 24,000 feet. Nearby, another range of jagged peaks sprinkled with snow shut out the view to the south. Undulating grassland stretched away to the east, while to the south-west I could see golden-brown patches of bog and the glitter of water. It was probably the finest view I had ever seen in my life.

We descended to the valley of Rich Gul down the stony, grass-covered mountainside, patched with golden bog-myrtle and other shrubs turned to a flaming red. The stones in the beds of streams we passed had been laid flat by glaciers which had long since dispersed. Continuing down the Rich Gul, we passed small stands of birch wherever streams flowed down the hillside and in one of these coppices we camped for the night.

At dawn the next day we were making our way in the cold shadows along the grassy hillside through more clusters of birch. Light and graceful trees, their leaves by now had turned to pure gold. Streams of foaming water, the icy melt from the snow peaks high above, rushed past us; numbingly cold like the Rich Gul which we later had to ford thigh-deep.

We then came to a most spectacular gorge framing a snow range 20,000 feet high. Here we had to carry the loads down as the path was very steep. Jahangir Khan annoyed me by taking only a 10-pound bag of flour. The rest of us were each carrying some 60 pounds. On a mountain, Jahangir was like a sick old woman allowed out for the first time.

We recrossed the river by a bridge and then stopped for lunch at 11, where the valley began to open out. Here, glacier-fed streams mingled with the river; high granite precipices rose very sheer above us; and, opposite, across the Rich Gul, were the towering snow peaks.

Further down the wide, boulder-strewn valley we crossed the river again by a bridge. Soon after this, we saw some cultivation and a few houses on the south bank, and then some more on our side. Recrossing the river by another bridge, we passed through a number of farms until we reached the Hakim's house an hour before nightfall.

I thought the Hakim of Rich a rather fine-looking old man. He arranged for beds and carpets to be put in an orchard, where we slept, and gave us quite a good dinner, besides some apples, apricots, melons and a few grapes. This neighbourhood, from the last bridge to beyond the Hakim's house, is all known as Rich. Downstream, according to Schomberg, the river is called the Turikho. The only difficulty here was getting firewood.

The following morning the Hakim gave us a good breakfast and we did not start off until after 8 AM, as I wanted to take some photographs. On the outer wall of the Hakim's house were four good ibex heads which I was told were from the Shah jin Ali; I heard that brown bear were also found nearby.

After Khunkhut, we wasted a lot of time bringing the animals over the shoulder of a mountain, but this was compensated by good views of the mountains further up the valley. We reached Shagram, the next village, late in the afternoon. Like all these villages, Shagram consisted of scattered farmsteads, each with its fields, hedges and orchards. Here the villagers had built several small, stonework dams across channels of the river, to make flight pools for duck-shooting. The Hakim, a friendly, distinguished-looking elderly man, whose name was Purdum Khan, seemed rather put out that we had not sent word on ahead; however, he installed us in a comfortable rest-house and brought us masses of fruit: peaches, pears, apples, melons and grapes.

We stayed on at Shagram until after lunch the next day. We

were given two meals: pieces of chicken and poached eggs, served in a rather tasteless soup, with rice or bread.

The rest of the day stayed rather hazy and a strong south-west wind got up towards the evening. Having started from Shagram at 12.30, we arrived at Rain soon after 2 PM, where the Hakim insisted on lending me his horse. We spent the remainder of the day here, and stayed the night as guests of an official named Doran; judging by the seven ibex heads adorning the verandah pillars of his house, this man was evidently a keen shikari. He told us he had shot all these ibex near Uzhnu, just above Khunkhut.

We left Rain soon after sunrise and continued down the river to Warkop, a prosperous-looking village, where there was a bridge. On the way downstream we passed several tombs, some of them enclosed by small rectangular buildings like summer houses. In this region, passers-by never stopped at these tombs to recite a prayer, whereas in Swat, everyone did so.

Coming from the bridge at Warkop to Zondrangram, we crossed a bare, waterless hillside, then a few inhabited cottages where the Tirich stream joined the Rich Gul, and after that a succession of farms where there were orchards of apple, apricot, peach and mulberry set among poplars, walnut trees and willows.

At Zondrangram, I saw numbers of idiot children and many villagers suffering from goitre. The villagers brought water to their cultivations over long distances by means of aqueducts, raised on wooden stilts, built along the mountainside. A number of mud avalanches had occurred nearby; these looked fairly recent and might have resulted from earlier snow avalanches bringing down mud and earth.

*

We left Zondrangram at dawn and passed Suich where there was a bridge. About an hour's walk below Suich, we crossed the river. Along the Turikho we found plenty of bridges, well-constructed, of wickerwork instead of merely rough planks of brushwood, and strong enough to bear the weight of a laden pony.

Despite a gusty, refreshing breeze this proved to be a wearisome day, overcast, hot and stuffy, with occasional rumbles of thunder in the distance. Shortly after 2 PM we arrived at Bandok, a deserted village high up on the far side of the river. Until we reached Zondrangram, no one had apparently heard of Bandok which, I discovered, was only inhabited at certain times of the year when the locals brought their sheep, goats and cattle up from the valley to graze. Villagers living lower down also came up to gather firewood at Bandok where some juniper and other bushes grew along the stream nearby.

At 6.45 the next morning I went off with a local guide up a tributary which flowed into the main stream at Bandok from the south-west. We came over the shoulder of a hill and crossed some grassland past a herdsman's stone shelter; from here on, we climbed steadily up towards a small glacier. I had hoped for a view of Tirich Mir from a snow-ridge above the glacier, but had to turn back when the climbing became too difficult. The local who was with me had not been much use on a mountain, and spent his time trying to persuade me to turn back. In spite of this, I did succeed in climbing to about 14,000 feet. From this height I had a magnificent view, across the stream from our camp, of a sheer rock peak towering above the range north of Tirich Mir. This peak was too sheer for snow to lie, except in a few crannies, and the bare rock varied in colour from orange-pink to cream, banded with purple, an effect which, to me, appeared very impressive.

We left Bandok soon after I had got back to our camp and arrived again at Suich by the middle of the afternoon. There, I found two men who had been sent by the Hakim of Drasan to meet me. We spent the night camped in a courtyard with a verandah on three sides and a well on the other. The villagers entertained us with some lively singing and dancing after dinner.

The following day, shortly before nine after a steep, steady climb up the mountain behind Suich, we reached a wave-like, grassy plateau covered with stones, the 12,000-foot summit of the Zani-an Pass. Despite the hazy atmosphere, we had a tremendous view of our surroundings. To the north I could see the Shah jin Ali Pass; the snow range, south-west of Mastuj, which looked especially impressive; and Tirich Mir, which had earlier been rather overshadowed by the peak north of Bandok and had not looked its height.

An even steeper descent for two hours down the bare, grassy face of the mountain brought us to Drasan village, nestling among groves of walnut, poplar and apple trees, in a side valley above the Rich Gul. The Hakim of Drasan had told our guides to take us to a certain orchard. I sent one of the guides on ahead, but when we got there we found nothing ready and a message from the Hakim telling us that he was sick. We continued on down to the river for some distance and, after a fairly breathless climb to get across a valley tributary, arrived at Kosht where we spent the night.

We camped under a chenar tree near a large house owned by the Sharwal, which had several ibex horns nailed to its pillars and the usual assortment of muzzle-loading guns hanging on the walls. The Sharwal kept a falcon with grey-barred plumage, which I could not identify.

We set off from Kosht at first light on 24 September, and crossed the Rich Gul downstream from the village. We then followed the river and, after a short detour, avoiding the high ground, we carried on down a valley, where hills on both sides shut out the view, as far as Reshun.

Further down, at Barenis, the valley widened considerably and now, looking back, I could see the mountains above Bandok.

Below Barenis the river flowed in a deep cutting at the foot of some high cliffs. Many of the mountain slopes were deeply scarred by erosion, which had gouged a series of fantastic pinnacles and spurs out of the hillside. On jutting shelves at different levels all over the lower slopes opposite us, I noticed farms where rice, millet and a grass-like seed crop were being cultivated. The path now climbed uphill for about two miles, to get across a ravine coming in from the south, and beyond this dropped steadily down to Maroi, where we stayed the night in a small wayside shop.

The road from Maroi to Chitral was rather dull and uninteresting as far as Kaghozi, where we found a single house and a mosque in a very attractive setting. Setting off from Kaghozi after lunch, we reached Chitral at 3 P M after an unusually brisk walk of four and a half hours.

Chitral consisted of a single, long street of simple, open-fronted shops. Besides this street-bazaar, there was a fort, two ugly mosques whose design I found pretentious, the political agent's dwelling – a pleasant house built in the local style – and some bungalows. Around Chitral were farms and cultivations and, from the town, a good view up the valley to Tirich Mir.

I met the wazir, Azim Shah bu Din, an elder brother of Lieutenant-Colonel Khushwaqt-al-Mulk whom I had previously met at Mastuj; he put me up in a bungalow on the edge of the river, below the fort, where I was well looked after.

I was told that markhor were to be found further up the ravine which opened on Chitral from the west; and that a few bears, black as well as brown, also lived in the surrounding hills. When I arrived, the locals were busy catching and training hawks, including kestrels which they would use in two months' time for hunting red-legged partridges, known as chikhor. Schomberg's book, *Kafirs and Glaciers*, confirmed that the Chitralis caught wild falcons in the same way Arab falconers did on the Trucial coast.

Since leaving Saidu Sharif in Swat a month before, I had covered some 350 miles of mountainous country. No wonder that by the time I reached Chitral, I was leg-weary; during the last few days even a five-hundred-foot climb had been an effort.

The Black Kafirs, who called themselves Kalash Gum, lived in the three valleys of Brumboret, Rambor and Barir. People there still worshipped the old gods, grew grapes for wine, and set up carved wooden figures where they buried their dead. Their kinsmen across the border had been forcibly converted to Islam by Abd er Rahman, Amir of Afghanistan, at the end of the last century, and their land, once known as Kafiristan, was now called Nuristan, 'Land of Light'. Many of the Muslims living in Chitral were descendants of Red Kafir refugees who had fled from Kafiristan in 1897. Some years later I was to travel through Nuristan, but I am glad that I saw the people here as they once had been throughout Kafiristan.

After a few days' rest, I visited the Kafirs, accompanied by

Above: A typical Kurd. They invariably wore their weapons.

Below: One of the first Kurds I met at Haji Umran. These Kurds, just across the frontier, in Iraq, wore their tribal dress, whereas in Persia the Kurds had been obliged to wear European clothes.

Above: Nasser Hussain, a young Kurd, who was my constant companion on both my journeys in Kurdistan.

Below: This photograph of Sheik Mahmud, the most outstanding character I met in Kurdistan, was possibly the last one taken of him. He died only a few years afterwards.

The start of my journey from Swat towards the Kachi Kuni Pass into Chitral.

Above: Two of my men at
the top of the 16,000 foot
Kachi Kuni Pass.

Right: The top of the
Kachi Kuni Pass.

Left: Yarkhun valley below Lasht, looking east.

Right: The mountains on the west side of the Yarkhun river below Lasht among the upper reaches of the Chitral river.

Left: A boy riding a yak above Lasht.

Above: On top of the Shah jin Ali Pass, looking east. The snow mountains in the background are 22,000 feet high and are in the Hindu Kush.

Right: A boy we met near Boroghil.

Far right: Kafir woman in the Barir valley.

Left: Ghilzai Kuchi in the Maidan migrating down to Jalalabad and Pakistan for the winter.

Left: Osed Khel towers in Waziristan.

Below: A typical Chitrali bridge in the Rich Gul.

Right: Carved memorial figure in the Brumboret valley, Kafiristan.

Far right: Ghilzai Kuchi in the Maidan. Kuchi means nomad; it is not a tribal name.

Below right: Khaibar in its dramatic setting.

Rakaposhi, the mountain I had come so far to see.

Above: In the heart of the Karakorams, north of Baltit, capital of Hunza.

Overleaf: On the Karumbar glacier, looking down the Ishkoman valley.

Below: The route to Kashgar, beyond Khaibar.

Previous page: Under the Chilinji Pass, near Biatar, looking down on the glacier a long way below.

Above: On the way to Kashgar, beyond Khaibar.

Below: These Kirghiz, to me, brought with them the lure of Inner Asia and forbidden lands.

the political agent, Mir Ajam, who took me by jeep to Aijun, a Red Kafir village, which he assured me was the largest village in Chitral. From Aijun I continued on foot up a narrow valley where a stream of clear water flowed down from the north-west. The steep, rocky hillsides on both sides were covered with trees, among them a species of scrub oak with leaves like holly but recognizable as oak from its acorns. We crossed and recrossed the stream by bridges, each made of a single plank. After about an hour and a half, we turned up the valley of the Brumboret, the southernmost of two tributaries. The other tributary, above the Brumboret, was called Rambor.

We met many parties of men and boys bringing sacks of wal-nuts down to Aijun. They carried long poles for knocking down the walnuts, which they shelled on the spot.

Further up, in Brumboret, we came to a succession of farms and terraced fields of rice and Indian corn, both of which were being cut. I saw a great many walnut trees, besides other fruit trees and some very big mulberry trees.

The valley here was rather wider and more level, the hillsides steep and rocky with scrub oak and, above this, forests of pine and fir. The villages in Brumboret were inhabited by both Muslims and Black Kafirs. We stopped at Batrik where there were about a dozen well-built Black Kafir houses in a side valley. The men dressed like Muslims, but the Kafir women and small girls wore a distinctive head-dress ornamented with tiny shells. All the women and girls wore a dark-brown, loose garment girdled in round the waist.

I took a number of photographs of Kafir men, women and children and two carved wooden statues, about six feet high, where they had placed dead bodies. Corpses were laid out in wooden coffins and then taken to a corner of a field and left there to disintegrate above ground. The statues were apparently commemorative, but the people had no objection to moving them into a better light to be photographed, indeed they rather chucked them about. The façades of the Kafir houses were also decorated with some simple carving.

From Brumboret, the way to the valley of Barir led uphill by a very steep track through scrub oaks, then extensive forests of pine and deodar. I saw few birds here; some fresh droppings I noticed on the track were probably those of markhor. The descent to Barir was much steeper and in places the track was barely discernible.

At the foot of a narrow, rocky gorge we found some Kafir houses surrounded by fields of rice and millet, fruit trees and large vines. We rested here for about half an hour and devoured quantities of small, sweet-tasting, purple grapes picked from a vine which must have been thirty feet high. We then continued on down the valley to Gurru, where the houses appeared to hang from a steep hillside above the stream.

I found the Barir valley more attractive than Brumboret. The first group of houses we encountered had been occupied by Muslims as well as Kafirs, although I gathered that Kafirs predominated here. As usual, the recently converted Muslims were very regular with their calls to prayer. In and around Gurru, all the houses were owned by Kafirs. I noticed certain dissimilarities between these people and the Chitralis. For instance, unlike the Chitrali men and boys, none of the Kafirs or Muslims carried catapult bows and, instead of a funnel above the hearth, the smoke from their fires had no outlet but the door. The Kafir villages were, besides, rather dirty and at Gurru I counted about sixty bed-bugs in my sleeping-bag.

At Gurru I found eight wooden grave figures placed on a small cliff; the figures were about five feet high, smaller than the ones

I had seen the previous day. They represented human forms, naked except for a short, tasselled loin-cloth, and helmets of several different shapes. I noticed that some of the Kafirs also wore a tasselled blanket round their waists and tied over the shoulder, but they wore trousers under this.

Two of the grave figures had been placed in the shade and I took these down into a field to photograph them.

The political agent from Chitral met me at Gabiret, on the Chitral river, later that morning and took me to Drosh where I lunched with Colonel Iftikhar ed Din, Commander of the Chitral Scouts. The colonel, whose father, Brigadier Sir Hisam ed Din, I had met in Peshawar, was a keen shikari and fisherman; I liked him greatly. He resembled an English country gentleman of ancient family and military traditions who had served with distinction in a cavalry regiment. We inevitably discussed big game hunting and the colonel told me that an indigenous variety of wild sheep, known as urial, could be found on the far side of the mountain to the west of Chitral. One of the scouts, he informed me, had recently shot a snow leopard at Aijun. The colonel had three urial heads in his bungalow, besides a magnificent markhor head and two very good ibex.

I met several other officers, including Major Mir Badshah, commanding officer of the Mahsud battalion on the Lawerai Pass. The major was a remarkable man who had served in France and East Africa during the 1914–18 war; his father was the most important of the Mahsud maliks. I felt that the major commanded this battalion out of a sense of duty to his people.

After lunch the PA took me on up to the Mahsud battalion camp just under the Lawerai Pass. It was snowing slightly when we arrived. The country here was wild, with a fine view, and forested with pine and firs, tall, straight, massive trees which were the most impressive I had seen in Chitral. The jeep track was very steep and would remain so until the Mahsuds had finished the properly graded road which they were then building. While we were backing the jeep to get round a corner, some goats, disturbed by the noise of the revving engine, started a small avalanche directly above us. One large stone hit the running-board, another smashed the driving-mirror, and a third deeply dented the bonnet just in front of me. Any one of these stones might have killed us and I felt that we had had a lucky escape.

On 1 October I left the battalion camp and drove in a lorry with some of the Mahsuds to Dergei. On the way we stopped at Dir, where I slept in the rest-house, a place like a prison; John Dent had given me a letter of introduction to the Nawab, but he did not even bother to acknowledge it when I sent it to him.

Next morning we joined a convoy of half-a-dozen lorries bound for Dergei. The journey took more than ten hours: the authorities at Dir had tried to load a large packing-case on our lorry, for which there was no room; after we had refused, they held us up for an hour-and-a-half at the state frontier on the pretext of searching us for contraband. From Dergei, I travelled by bus to Peshawar, and stayed there for three nights with the Dents. While I was in Peshawar I tried to get a tooth pulled out which had been troubling me; but instead the dentist injected the inflamed gum surrounding it with penicillin.

I left Peshawar by bus at 10 A M and arrived six hours later at Bannu, where I spent the night with a missionary doctor called Iliffe, a very impressive person who had a great hold on the Mahsuds.

I went on by bus, over some arid sandy country, to Tank. Here the officer in command of the Khassadars took me on to

Serwakhai. Along the road I saw pickets of Khassadars; the officer told me that there were 2,800 of them in South Waziristan and 2,500 in the North. The Khassadars were recruited on a hereditary basis, hence their numbers included small boys and elderly men; they were paid fifty rupees a month, and alternated one month's leave with a month on duty.

We now headed for Wana accompanied by an armed escort we had picked up on the way to Serwakhai. The country became more open, undulating and somewhat less rugged; we passed many cemeteries beside the road, and tombs of holy men marked by long poles hung with white and red flags.

At Wana, the South Waziristan Scouts headquarters, we stayed the night with the PA, Attaullah Jan Khan, a man in his late forties; Jan Khan was a striking personality, intelligent, forceful and charming, with – I fancied – sound balance and judgement. The Commandant of the Scouts, Lieutenant Colonel Abd el Jabar, was said to be a first-rate soldier. Wana was a large camp in an open plain, with a perimeter far too extensive for the wing stationed there to hold in the event of trouble. We had tea with the high school staff and the boys, and that night we dined in the officers' mess.

Next morning, accompanied by a Khassadar officer, Captain Matab Shah, I visited the Khassadar pickets at Sholam, about ten miles across the plain north-west of Wana. I took a number of photographs of these Khassadars at Sholam, who were all Waziris. We had dinner with the boys' Company, smart, attractive-looking lads, and afterwards there was Khutwak dancing. Much of this consisted of spinning round and round very fast. The dancers, bare-headed with bobbed hair, were energetic and extremely graceful.

On 10 October I drove with Major Muhammad Akram to Tanai, where we picked up a troop of Mahsuds and rode with them on a *gasht* (a military operation) to Toi Khullah on the Wand Toi, a distance of twelve miles, but which took three hours. It was interesting to watch the Mahsuds picketing the small rocky hills on either side of us to protect the Powindah nomads passing through this area. The Powindah are migratory camel-owning tribes from Afghanistan who come down into Pakistan for the winter months, and then on to the Punjab. They surrendered their rifles at posts on the edge of the administered districts.

Next morning we set off at 7 AM with the Khassadar officer, Captain Shah, for Tiarza, two miles south of Torwam. The road climbed over some fair-sized hills, and from there we had a good view back across the Wana plain. I saw parties of Waziris moving down with their oxen and flocks of goats from the hills to the lower ground.

In the evening there was dancing, and while I thought the dancers less impressive than others I had seen at Wana, they performed some amusing skits – for instance, an Afghan general inspecting his troops – which showed that they were naturally gifted actors.

The next morning, a Scouts' bus picked me up and took me to Khajuri, on the Agency border. Khajuri lay in the Tochi, an open valley, unusually rich and well-cultivated for these parts, flanked on both sides by low hills. The valley was inhabited by the Dawar. Also, Waziris with strings of camels carried planks of wood from here to Bannu, which they sold in exchange for food.

The Khajuri fort with its gardens and trees, planted close to the walls, gave one the impression that it was less in the front-line than Wana.

*

Early the following morning I drove up the valley to the Khassadar fort at Boya. The hillsides here were covered with olive trees; we passed villages with watch-towers, and a fair amount of cultivation.

In the fort I took more photographs of the Waziri Khassadars before lunch and then drove down the Bannu road to the fork leading to Thal. Here we found two large Powindah encampments; with their small black tents pitched close together, surrounded by large herds of camels, from a distance they looked very like Bedu encampments. The Powindah seemed to be very well armed, but they were friendly and very ready to be photographed.

I left Miran Shah the next morning for Razmak with the Khassadar officer, the Agency surgeon and about a dozen Khassadars. The surgeon had the wind up properly, and did all he could to stop me visiting this abandoned British Army camp which had once been an important military frontier position. We crossed the river near Isha and collected some more Khassadars to picket the road. From here we climbed fairly steeply towards oak forests. Near Osed Khel, we passed several groups of women driving laden cattle and small flocks of goats; the women carried rifles and were only joined at night by the men, because they all had blood feuds and consequently hid during the day. No-one would molest the women, however, who were only armed in order to protect their flocks.

Nearly every house we passed had a high watch-tower built in the middle of the courtyard; these towers were never positioned on the courtyard wall, which had an overhang of brushwood to deter intruders and no outer windows.

We stopped for some tea at Dorsali, a Scout fort now occupied by Khassadars, and from there we drove along the valley, past more towered houses, terraced fields and hillsides thickly forested with oak, fir and juniper. The road then wound up to a pass which led to the Razmak plateau.

Razmak was a depressing place. The camp itself had suffered little damage, but in the cantonment I found a waste of uniform, tin-roofed, concrete bungalows with shattered window-panes, overgrown gardens and unkempt lawns. A ruined Mogul fort would have looked impressive and probably beautiful, whereas the disused modern buildings of a formerly British cantonment such as this looked neglected and hideous. The only occupants appeared to be a few Khassadars, some boys herding small flocks of goats and an old, decrepit donkey. We motored briefly round the camp and then left, since we wanted to get back to Miran Shah before news of our arrival at Razmak was received in the nearby villages.

I spent the night at Miran Shah, and travelled the next day to Bannu. On the way we stopped at another large encampment of Powindahs, near Khajuri, where I took many more photographs. At Bannu I stayed again with the Iliffes, and on 17 October I arrived back in Peshawar.

HUNZA

1953

THE FOLLOWING YEAR I again spent the hot weather in Pakistan. I flew from Basra to Karachi, arriving there on 6 August 1953. In Karachi I stayed with Martin and Monica Moynihan, from the British High Commission, whose kind hospitality helped me to endure a thoroughly frustrating month in this unattractive city. The Prime Minister had sanctioned my proposed journey through Gilgit and Hunza, but was then deliberately obstructed by the Minister for Kashmir Affairs whose office issued the permits. After a row between them in Cabinet, I was eventually given the necessary papers.

From Karachi I went to Peshawar where I engaged a bearer, an English-speaking Pathan called Faiz Muhammad, and I drew more money which, for convenience, I divided into small denominations; I also purchased a small supply of tinned food. Leaving Peshawar, we travelled by bus and jeep, by way of Natiagalli, where I spent the night with John Dent, to Batakondie. At Batakondie I hired two mules to take us up the Kagan valley and over the Babusar Pass.

On 9 September we left Batakondie after midday and marched for eight miles to Burawai, situated at 10,000 feet in an open valley with bare, grassy hillsides and a few scattered pine trees.

The following morning, near Besal, we came across a large

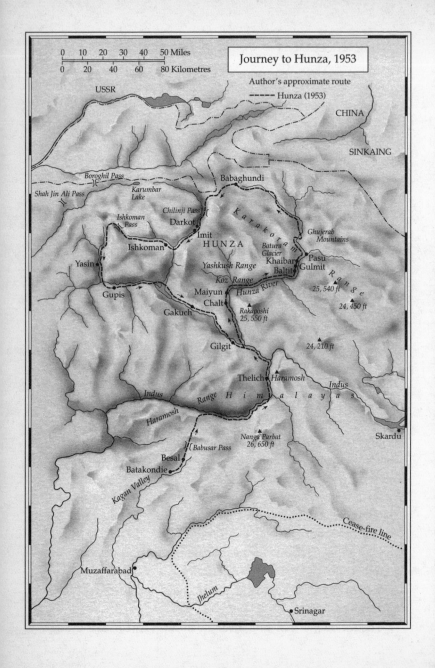

Journey to Hunza, 1953

Author's approximate route
— · — Hunza (1953)

USSR

CHINA

SINKAING

Boroghil Pass

Shah Jin Ali Pass

Karumbar Lake

Babaghundi

Chilinji Pass

Ishkoman Pass

Darkot

Imit

HUNZA

Karakoram

Ghujerab Mountains

Ishkoman

Yashkush Range

Batura Glacier

Khaibar

Pasu

Yasin

Koz Range

Baltit

Gulmit

Range

Gupis

Maiyun

Hunza River

25,540 ft

Chalt

Gakuch

Rakaposhi
25,550 ft

24,450 ft

24,210 ft

Gilgit

Thelich

Haramosh

Indus

Range

Himalayas

Indus

Skardu

Haramosh

Nanga Parbat
26,650 ft

Babusar Pass

Besal

Batakondie

Kagan Valley

Cease-fire line

Muzaffarabad

Jhelum

Srinagar

encampment of Gujur tribesmen with flocks of sheep and goats, buffaloes, cattle, donkeys and some horses. Until Partition these nomads had always wintered in Jammu. Their black tents had built-up walls made of stones. The men were fine-looking but dirty; most of them wore black or white turbans, duffle-coloured shirts and pyjamas. The children's faces were filthy. Other Gujurs were on the move along the track with their animals. A few of their women, draped completely in white with lattice-work veils, rode on horses or mules; most of them, unveiled and with their hair braided in plaits, went on foot.

After walking for almost twenty miles, I felt tired and foot-weary by the time we reached Gitadas, the frontier constabulary post, late in the afternoon. I thought the Kagan valley disappointing after all I had heard of it. There had been no really fine views and nowhere did I find the scenery truly impressive.

The next day, a steady climb for about two hours brought us to the top of the Babusar Pass from where we had a good view of Nanga Parbat, and another clear view, down the valley towards Gilgit, of the Haramosh range. Some melted snow gave us water and we lunched on the 14,000-foot summit, basking in warm sunshine among blue gentians and patches of deep-red moss.

The descent from the pass was very rapid. We were soon down among firs and pines, where caravans of camels and mules were camped among the trees. In Babusar I found a lot of ugly, European-style houses which resembled those of a Welsh mining village.

From the pass to the Indus valley, the track descended 12,000 feet in twenty-four miles. We left Babusar village at sunrise and came down through the fir woods, past log cabins and plantations of millet, walnuts, vines and apple trees. We halted at noon close to Dasar, on the pleasant, grassy bank of a rivulet shaded by an overhanging willow; then, after an hour's rest and a meal, we carried on down a desolate valley to the Indus, which was sluggish here and smaller than I had expected.

Climbing again from the Indus valley we arrived at Chelas, 3,000 feet up on a bare, stony plateau. Since neither mules nor porters were available at Chelas, I had to wait here for three days for a jeep.

Despite a cloudy start to the day, which prevented me from getting a clear view of Nanga Parbat, I greatly enjoyed the drive up the Indus valley to Gilgit. North of Thelich, especially, I thought the valley most impressive. The Indus, a dirty brownish-grey in colour, flowed through a fine gorge and the barren mountains, shaded umber, brown and rust, were awe-inspiring in their austerity. To me the scenery was infinitely more attractive than that of the much-vaunted Kagan valley. High up on the mountainsides, above the pine and juniper, were birches whose leaves had already turned golden. Markhor, ibex and urial were all common in this area. Urial inhabited the gentler, lower slopes; markhor and ibex the bare, rocky terrain higher up.

We stopped for an hour at Thelich to drink some tea and eventually reached Gilgit late in the afternoon. I had a letter of introduction from John Dent to Khan Muhammad Jan Khan, the political agent at Gilgit, who was cheerful and friendly and put me up in the Northern Scouts' mess.

Instead of a town, Gilgit turned out to be more of a straggling, cultivated area about four miles in extent, set in a barren valley with bare mountains rising steeply on both sides of the river. Houses stood in their own gardens and orchards, surrounded by cultivated fields, against a backdrop of the distant, snow-covered Haramosh peaks. The bazaar consisted of a long, straight street of adjoining shops shaded by trees.

On 18 September Faiz Muhammad and I left Gilgit with a local man and two pack-horses. We travelled along the valley of the Hunza river, in places over soft sand where the going was heavy. It was also rather hot. Like the Indus, the Hunza river was coloured a dirty, brownish-grey by quantities of silt. A few tamarisk grew on the valley floor. We made good progress, seventeen miles in six hours, and arrived at Nomal, the first village after Gilgit, at two in the afternoon.

We were off again at sunrise, marching along under over-hanging mountains whose barren, rocky slopes, apart from scattered conifers and juniper, were almost devoid of vegetation. I now had my first glimpses of Rakaposhi, the brilliant white snow mantling its shoulders contrasting with a cloudless, deep blue sky.

Another three hours' walking brought us to Chalt, an attractive village set among poplars, fruit trees and terraced fields of rice at the end of a bare stretch of the valley. We bought some excellent grapes here from a donkey-caravan loaded with panniers from Hunza, and spent the night in the rest-house at the far end of the village.

Leaving Chalt at first light, we had to make a detour to get to the bridge over a wide stream flowing down from a large valley on our left. From here Rakaposhi, 25,550 feet high, dominated everything. It was a magnificent mountain, a great white pyramid of ice, towering over its surroundings. We had an unbroken view of the whole side of the mountain which was now right over our heads.

For the next three days we could see this incredible mountain rising abruptly from the far side of the great valley up which we travelled. I remembered Shipton describing Rakaposhi in the Travellers' Club, and how this had fired me with desire to see it. Now I had done so: whatever lay ahead, the journey had been worthwhile.

We passed through a succession of orchards and farmsteads clinging on to the lower slopes of the mountains above cliffs that fell sheer to the river. Rivulets of cold, dirty-grey glacier water, with snow-crystals swirling in it, irrigated the fields. Everyone we met saluted us and seemed very friendly. Some lads carrying panniers of fruit to Gilgit gave us excellent peaches, and in one place the villagers brought us delicious grapes which we stopped to eat at leisure. At Maiyun, ten miles beyond Chalt, we rested for a couple of hours. Rakaposhi loomed directly above us, but was rather foreshortened from this angle so that one of its lower peaks looked higher than the actual summit.

The path from Maiyun to Hindi wound round the barren shoulder of a mountain for two or three miles. We reached Hindi at 4 PM and spent the night in the Mir's dak bungalow. Here we saw extensive areas of cultivation: millet, rice, vegetables, hemp, a grain crop called *bajra*, and *trumba*, whose heavy-scented, pale-pinkish-white flowers produced small, black, edible seeds. The village headman and several other notables were there to welcome us when we arrived, and a crowd of small boys, some of them carrying catapult-bows like the two-stringed bows I had seen in Chitral. The men in this area, too, wore cloaks similar to those worn by the Chitralis.

I stayed on at Hindi until the sun was on Rakaposhi, so that I could photograph it. From here, the track to Aliabad and Baltit led through fields and orchards. Rakaposhi was in sight for most of the time, and I had a good view of the high snow peaks, from Aliabad, up the Hunza river valley beyond the Hispar glacier. We reached Karimabad, the Mir's residence just below his old residence at Baltit, soon after midday. The scenery here was superb: Rakaposhi, the snow peaks of Hispar and the snow-covered, bare, sheer-sided mountain rising straight up behind the village. The slopes above the Hunza river were covered with terraced fields, farms and orchards. There were no markhor, I was told, this side of Chalt, and no black bear, but numbers of ibex, urial, brown bear and snow leopard. *Ovis poli*, a variety of wild sheep named after Marco Polo, were found near the Mantaka Pass, at the Sinkiang border on the road to Kashgar.

I lunched with the Mir of Baltit, a very friendly man with a strong personality, who spoke excellent English; and that evening I dined with him at his house where we were joined by Lady Noon, the Australian wife of the Governor of the Punjab, and her companions who had just arrived from Gilgit on holiday: The Mir told me that the Shah of Persia's brother had recently passed through Baltit on a shooting trip. He was now in the Afghan Pamirs where he had shot an *Ovis poli* with 62-inch horns. The prince was a keen shikari, but everywhere had made himself disliked by his arrogance and bad manners. The Mir confessed that he could not stand him.

The sky next morning was overcast and stormy-looking and I hoped that the weather was not going to break. I spent some of the day reading *China to Chitral*, written by Eric Shipton's friend and fellow-mountaineer, H. W. Tilman. Bill Tilman had just managed to get over the 17,000-foot Chilinji Pass, but was turned back by the weather at Karumbar late in October. From his account the journey was hard going. We would travel with ponies from Baltit to Reshit and, from there, with yaks over the Chilinji Pass to Karumbar, Darkot and Yasin.

We left at 6.45 A M with two ponies carrying our loads. The track from Baltit descended steeply into the narrow valley, past the fort at the mouth of the gorge. From there on, up the valley, it wound up and down the bare, precipitous cliffs above the river, in places built out on ledges of rock projecting from the sheer mountainside. Just before Gulmit, we passed a rope bridge suspended about forty feet above the river. The bridge was like a stretched-out ladder, with its footway made of wooden rungs and a rope handrail on either side; I saw several people crossing the river by this bridge but I doubted if I could have brought myself to go across it. We stopped for the night at Gulmit, a fair-sized village larger than most other villages in these parts, from which I had a view of the Ghujerab mountains beyond the Shimshal river: jagged, powdered with snow, glimpsed through the clouds against a bright blue sky.

After some arguments with the ponymen about their wages, we set off from Gulmit at daybreak up the bare shoulder of the mountain. To begin with, the ponies' loads kept slipping and in one place both bolted, scattering our baggage all over the hillside. After this we proceeded very slowly. It took us nearly four hours to reach the next village, Pasu, a distance of only seven miles, where we crossed the snout of a small glacier and halted for a meal among the fields and orchards which covered a fair area of the valley floor.

From Pasu we crossed a flat, sandy, gravel plain about two miles in extent, and then climbed steeply to the edge of the Batura glacier. The glacier was a tumbled mass of boulders, stones and earth with the underlying ice visible only in a few crevasses. It looked impracticable for our ponies, but we picked a way across with some difficulty. The jagged pinnacles of the sheer-sided Ghujerab mountains looked very impressive from here, their colours varying from pale orange, rust and umber to slate grey. Looking back across the tumbled mass of the glacier, I could see the high, snow-covered mountains between Hispar and the Shimshal and, up the valley, snow peaks of the Batura range above Khaibar.

A steep climb from the far side of the glacier, followed by an equally steep descent to the valley bottom, brought us eventually to Khaibar, a tiny village set in an amphitheatre of barren mountains. There were threshing floors in front of the houses and yaks grazed on the sunlit slopes above the village. Khaibar, in its dramatic setting, was one of the most attractive places I had yet seen, and I also liked the people.

In the morning we started off later than usual, as I wished to take some photographs and the sun had been a long time rising from behind the mountain opposite Khaibar. For the first two hours there were endless delays due to slipping loads. In one place, where the track, though steep, had been perfectly good, one of the ponies fell for no apparent reason. Luckily, this did not happen where the track was very narrow and built out over the river.

The scenery was dominated by the massive Ghujerab mountains which dwarfed everything else around them. With snow-covered peaks and a dusting of recent snow on their lower slopes, they rose straight up over our heads; in this weather, they looked dark and indescribably barren.

Beyond a bridge where the Misgar road crossed the river, the country became more open, the mountainsides sloping more gently and the going now easier for the ponies and ourselves alike. In the early afternoon we reached Khudabad. For the last three miles, before we got to the village, we had passed an odd farmstead or two among its fields and orchards; then came the headman's house and Khudabad, perched on a cliff above the river.

This was a good day for photography; fine and sunny with effective masses of cloud. Until now we had passed very few travellers since leaving Gilgit, but today we encountered a party with loaded yaks, one of the men wearing the same kind of 'admiral's' hat I had seen the previous year at Boroghil.

The headman's house, where we stayed the night, was clean and pleasant.

The following day we marched for about eight hours as far as Kirmin. Rather than the wild, dark, sheer-sided mountain peaks, flecked with snow, here the blending colours of gentler scree-slopes lower down – cream, buff, old ivory and dove-grey – made the scenery.

All morning the sky had been a deep, pure blue without a cloud in sight, but in the afternoon it clouded over. By the evening a cold gale was blowing and the clouds were low down over the mountains.

The track climbed several times 1,000 to 2,000 feet round shoulders of the mountains only to drop again into the river-bed but, despite this, the going was good and the gradients easy. Near one of the terraced villages we passed a shrine encircled by a rough stone wall, decorated with white flags on poles. Inside this enclosure I saw two large piles of ibex horns, all of them small.

Kirmin, like other villages in Hunza, consisted of scattered groups of single-storeyed, flat-roofed houses built of stones and earth. The villagers were ploughing their fields when we arrived. Here everything seemed very expensive. In the end I bought a young sheep for twelve rupees. Chickens, I was told, cost three rupees.

The following morning there was almost a brawl when the villagers tried to force me to take their ponies on from here, the only time I experienced any trouble.

From Kirmin, the going was easy along the valley to Reshit where we stopped for an early lunch. Reshit was quite a small village; unlike every other village I had seen so far, the houses were built close together so that you entered it through narrow streets. Usually the villages in Hunza, like those in Swat and Chitral, consisted of scattered farmsteads.

In contrast to the mud-grey waters of the Indus, here the river was coloured a milky green. Some parts of the valley below Reshit had been cultivated; the remainder of it consisted of marshy pools. A few ibex horns I noticed on the roof of the village mosque indicated that there were no large ibex in this neighbourhood.

At Spanj, Faiz Muhammad and I paid off the two ponymen and engaged four porters and two yaks. We loaded the yaks – the porters would take over when we reached the formidable Chilinji Pass. The yaks moved maddeningly slowly, making perhaps two miles an hour. Every now and then, feeling skittish, one or other would prance about with its tail in the air: never in my life have I seen anything so ridiculous.

The Yashkuk stream, which we forded soon after leaving Spanj, ran thigh-deep and felt numbingly cold. Muhammad Aziz, the headman of Reshit, met us two miles from Babaghundi and gave us salt-tea, curds, cream and some good bread. He and some other men accompanied us to Babaghundi. He gave me a yak to ride which I steered by a rope threaded through its nose, brought back over its head between its horns.

I found the yak a comfortable mount, sure-footed but too slow.

A bitterly cold wind was blowing by the time we reached Babaghundi. I took refuge from the cold in an empty house, sheltered by some willows, beside a rocky hillock crowned with a ruined fort near the village shrine. The shrine consisted of a small timber-roofed building surrounded by a low stone wall. It was decorated with many flags, mostly white; a great number of ibex horns, some very large, were piled in a monumental heap outside. An area nearby had been reserved for prayer and beyond this were some rooms for the use of the shrine's guardian. Apart from the guardian, at the time I arrived, Babaghundi was deserted.

Clouds shrouding the higher ground above the valley gave me occasional glimpses of the purple, orange and mauve-coloured cliffs powdered with snow. The weather looked lowering and unsettled for our crossing of the Chilinji Pass.

Just before sunset, three Kirghiz turned up on yaks, the advance party of a caravan going to Spanj to buy flour. They wore dark clothes, thickly padded; two had black fur caps, and the other an eared cap of leopard skin. Drab, uncouth figures riding strange beasts, they had come down from the passes of the north; to me they brought the lure of Inner Asia and forbidden lands.

At 7 AM we set off again with our yaks and porters, along the river past groves of willow and thorn, a small-leafed variety with a red berry. We met three more Kirghiz with four yaks, part of the caravan heading for Spanj, from whom we bought some ghee which was solid like lard and wrapped, like sausages, in intestines. Whereas the Kirghiz we had met the previous night were all middle-aged, these three were young men with flattish, Mongolian faces.

The track continued along the mountainside before descending to the river which here dwindled to a stream. We forded the stream, then crossed the moraine of a glacier and rounded the shoulder of another mountain to Biatar, at the foot of the Chilinji Pass, where we camped in two rough shelters built under overhanging rocks. The scenery between Babaghundi and Biatar had been very striking, dominated by high snow peaks of the Yashkush and Koz ranges. A lot of juniper and wild roses grew along the mountainsides, besides some yellow daisies; earlier in the season, there must have been a lot of flowers here.

At Biatar, some villagers from Spanj turned up who had been trying unsuccessfully to shoot ibex.

Here among the mountains I found that I slept very little. Most of the night I would doze on an imperceptible line between sleep and waking, yet in the morning I would feel quite rested. This night at the foot of the pass had been no exception. I rose and made tea at 4 A M, but could not get the porters under way until after five.

Despite a cloudy start to the day, the weather looked promising. We brought the yaks as far as the shoulder of the mountain, but we had to abandon them where a rocky defile proved too narrow for them to pass, even without their loads. In this arctic landscape there seemed nothing for them to eat, but the porters assured me that the yaks would scratch about and find enough beneath the snow, and be all right until they came back for them. The porters now carried loads of about 60 pounds apiece, together with their own rations.

Beyond this point the going was reasonably easy, much of it up a glacier. Ploughing upwards, knee-deep, through the snow, I was worried about crevasses but the porters appeared unconcerned; they trudged steadily ahead and rested often. We reached the top of the pass at one o'clock and rested there a while, gazing over range upon range of mountains, some in heavy shadow, all of which Tilman, who had crossed the Chilinji Pass some years before, had described as looking 'eminently unclimbable'.

But we had to get down into the valley before night fell. Immediately beneath us was a very steep slope of snow-covered scree. At first glance it looked impassable, but luckily the snow was soft and we slipped and slithered down for 2,000 feet, falling frequently. Had the snow been frozen I do not think we should have ever got down.

The porters were exhausted by the time we reached the bottom and Faiz was in equally poor shape. However, I felt hardly tired and took a load and went on with Mirza Khan, the strongest of my party, as we had to get to the 'jungle' in the valley below for firewood. After the very steep 2,000-foot slope the going was easy until we came to the last 1,000 feet which were steep and rocky.

By the late afternoon Mirza and I arrived in the 'jungle', the upper fringes of a belt of willow extending down into the valley; here there was abundant firewood. The others eventually struggled in and hot tea and a meal soon had everybody happy. We made a huge fire and slept round it on rather rocky ground under the stars.

The next day, I delayed setting off until the porters had mended the soles of their soft leather boots which were much the worse for wear after the previous day's scramble. The day was cold and cheerless with flurries of snow at intervals.

On the cliffs around us we heard ibex (which the porters called markhor) whistling continually, a bird-like note rather like a curlew. Also a lot of chikhor were calling on the mountain tops.

We saw tracks of ibex everywhere on our way down the valley. We followed a stream whose banks were clothed with thickets of golden birch and willow. The mountains around us were shrouded in mist; when we camped at midday, we chose a place where a jutting rock would give us shelter if it snowed. I decided to go to Ishkoman from here, and then to Darkot, instead of Boroghil, where if the weather broke we could not hope to get across the Darkot Pass. In any case, I had already seen the country beyond Karumbar the previous year.

It snowed throughout the night and for the whole of the next day. About three feet of snow had fallen by the time we started and visibility was down to fifty yards. We struggled through the deep snow down the valley for a mile and a half to an overhanging rock with a low cave under it. The cave was nowhere more than three feet high and in consequence the smoke was troublesome when we lit a fire. We stayed there for the rest of the day; I slept in my tent away from the smoke.

The following morning we started early and struggled down to the main valley again through deep snow which made it difficult to pick a way through large boulders. The weather, however, was now clear and bright. The juniper and birch were laden with snow. For a mile or two we followed the tracks of a snow leopard which had chosen the easiest route. Then we crossed the stream and halted in a forest of large, blasted juniper on a terrace above the river below some high, precipitous cliffs. Here an Uzbek had built two or three rough log cabins round the juniper trees. He had large flocks of sheep and goats, a few small black cows and a couple of large, well-kept, friendly dogs. He was out hunting when we arrived but turned up later and seemed very hospitable. He gave us excellent curds, butter with bread and a meat stew for lunch. The Uzbek was a refugee from Russia who had been living in India for the past twenty years. He had bought this patch of forest three years ago. His family included two or three small boys and some women whom we did not see.

We spent an extremely pleasant day with the Uzbek; the sun was hot but all the time it was freezing hard in the shade. Beyond his encampment was a thick wood of golden birch and a fine view of the Chilinji Pass and the high peaks above it, and on the other side of the valley.

A Kirghiz arrived on a horse very heavily laden with sacks of flour. He was on his way back to the Pamirs but, because of the weather, would probably have to remain here for another week or two. In the evening two Wakhis, servants of our Uzbek host, turned up with a small flock of goats. They had just returned from the Pamirs and told us that the snow there was waist-deep.

That night we had an enormous fire of juniper branches. I bought a sheep for twelve rupees, and after dinner the men danced round the fire to tunes which one of our porters played skilfully on a pipe. Despite a very hard frost I slept snugly in my two flea-bags on the snow at some distance from the fire to avoid the sparks, which are bad with juniper wood.

I rose to the sound of ibex whistling on the cliffs above our camp; we were to see many of them further on. We crossed the river again and followed it downstream through thickets of juniper, willow, wild rose and birch, under sheer cliffs of bare rock which disappeared into the clouds thousands of feet above us. Occasionally stones came rattling down as the mountainside warmed in the sun. After we had forded the river a second time, we had some difficulty crossing another fast-flowing torrent, over frozen rocks. Faiz waded the torrent in his boots which made me angry; I told him this was just the way to do his feet in properly.

We halted briefly at Buk, near some hovels; then we crossed the main river again and carried on over the jumbled moraine of a glacier, along a wide, gloomy, boulder-strewn valley to Matramza.

Two of the Hunza porters went back from Matramza, leaving behind Mirza, the eldest, and Latif, the youngest, who remained with me throughout the rest of the journey. We hired a pony to carry the other two loads and leaving the village we crossed the snout of the Karumbar glacier, a chaos of tumbled rocks, stones, earth and dirty blackish-grey ice. The glacier, rising from the 25,000-foot Batura mountains north-west of Baltit, virtually barricaded the valley. A fair-sized stream gushed out from beneath the ice.

We had to pick our way over the debris of two smaller glaciers before we reached Balhan near Bad Swat, a large terraced settlement further up the valley. By mid-afternoon low cloud had blotted out the view up the main glacier, and a storm of wind and rain broke soon after we arrived at the village. I found the inhabitants of Bad Swat welcoming and hospitable. The Wazir's son, a boy of about seventeen, turned up at sunset by which time the storm had abated.

Next morning we continued on to Imit, quite a small village attractively positioned in the Ishkoman valley. Except for some houses and cultivated fields, Ishkoman itself was in ruins; the Mir, Sultan Ghazi, now lived permanently at Imit where there was a small mosque and a guest-house. On the way along the valley I had seen a peregrine falcon and here, for the first time, I saw many smaller birds, mostly warblers. The Mir kept a sparrow-hawk which he used for hunting partridges; he was very friendly and provided us with fruit and other food.

The Ishkoman Pass was only 14,000 feet high, but the Mir warned me that after the recent snow we might find it impassable, so I decided to engage four extra porters to help us carry our loads over the pass. I planned to spend the following night on the near side of the pass and arrive at Darkot the day after that.

The Mir and some of his retainers accompanied us for about two miles, as far as the river which we crossed with the help of their ponies. We went up a side valley to a small village, beyond the ruins of Ishkoman, where we exchanged the pony we had brought from Matramza for four porters.

Higher up the valley, we came to a forest of juniper, where many large branches had been broken by the weight of snow. In several villages, I saw houses built like wigwams, of tree trunks and large branches, some of them with a rough stone wall round the bottom. After seven hours' march, we eventually arrived at a deserted village on the snow-line. This village was only occupied during the summer, so there were four or five empty houses now, in one of which we slept.

We kept a fire burning all night but even so, by morning, some water which had been left in a cup within two feet of the fire was frozen over.

Starting at sunrise we went up the south side of the valley where the snow lay about a foot deep. The porters went slowly with constant halts. After about three hours we reached the last of the trees. The porters wanted to camp here and cross the pass the next day, saying it was a very long way to the top. I refused and insisted on going on as I was afraid the weather might break; true, it showed no signs of doing so, being a perfect, cloudless day, but from experience I knew that it could cloud over without warning. Besides, everyone we asked had assured us that we could get to Darkot that same day. From where we were to the top of the pass looked close and easy; I expected to reach the summit by noon.

We now got on to a flat, snow-covered plain about three miles across. This proved heavy going, the snow being about eighteen inches deep, and it took us two hours to cross it. Beyond this came a succession of ascents and depressions, none of them very steep, but heavy going through two or three feet of snow.

The top of the pass remained elusive. We climbed up to what I had taken to be the top, only to have to work all the way back to our right, towards what looked like yet another summit, and then back again behind a rocky ridge to our left. The last stage consisted of a series of steep ascents and descents into small, snow-covered basins. In places the snow lay waist-deep.

Mirza and I went on ahead to break a trail while the porters lagged behind leaving us uncertain of the road, and Faiz Muhammad, who was nearly in tears, set the porters a rotten example by sitting down after every few steps.

The sun had disappeared over the ridge and by now it was getting very cold. We finally struggled to the last crest at 5.15 PM, about half an hour before sunset. On the snow near the summit I noticed a single comatose fly.

On the far side was a steep, snow-covered descent. The porters warned us to keep well to our right, off the glacier and clear of any crevasses. Again Mirza and I led the way. Faiz, now in tears and almost hysterical, begged me to stop and sleep where we were but I told him and the porters that we must get down to the 'jungle'.

At the top of the pass I noticed some large tracks but had been too preoccupied to pay them any attention. When I asked Mirza what they were he said they were the fresh tracks of a very large brown bear. The sight of them had a considerable effect in getting the porters down the hill.

The going was difficult; in some places I broke through more than waist-deep. Mirza and I went on ahead with Latif as a connecting link with the porters. At about 7.30 PM we stopped, having lost touch with Latif. Mirza was all for pushing on down to the 'jungle', but this I refused to do until I had established contact with the others, angry that even if we went on we stupidly had no matches with us to light a fire. Mirza finally disappeared and I was left by myself on the frozen mountainside, half expecting to have to sleep on the snow without any covering. I called and called and after about an hour heard an answering shout, so started back uphill. Suddenly the four porters loomed out of the night. They said Faiz had bedded down under a rock and that Latif was with him. Since there were two of them and Faiz had ample bedding with him and Latif an overcoat and a cloak I was not worried. I therefore went on slowly downhill with the four porters, trying to pick the best way by starlight. Owing to the snow there was quite a lot of light.

We came to one frighteningly steep face which never seemed to end, but the snow was crisp and frozen and held well, and eventually we got down to the bottom. I then found that one of the porters had stayed at the top behind a rock. I knew I could never get back up to fetch him, so went on down to the stream with the other three. After going some way along the stream we came to a little scattered shrub and some rough sheepfolds. It was after midnight by the time the porters lit a fire and I crawled into my sleeping bags. Lying awake, I knew that I had made a mess of things by ignoring local advice.

During the night the snow melted through my sleeping bags. I had taken off my trousers and socks which were lumps of ice and my feet remained very cold. I stayed where I was till the sun reached me, then I gave the three porters a tin of bully beef and tea (Mirza had the sugar with him) and I made myself some Bovril. We stayed where we were, drying our things and getting warm, until 10 AM. The missing porter meanwhile turned up at 8.30 AM. I then took the porters down the valley for about three miles to an empty village, within sight of Darkot, where we found Mirza. His feet were slightly frost-bitten. He would have done better to have stayed with me. We had a cup of tea and then, taking my pack with my sleeping bags, groundsheet and some tinned food, I started back up the hill to look for Faiz and Latif. I was nearly back at our last night's stopping place when I found them. Latif was all right, but Faiz's feet were a little frost-bitten.

As we approached the village where I had spent the night we met three locals who had heard we were missing and were coming to our assistance. We had some more tea and then went down to their village about two miles away. The headman was most hospitable and insisted on slaughtering a sheep for us, despite our protests.

I was now able to relax and take in the surroundings. The views were magnificent, especially down the valley beyond Darkot, to some very fine snow mountains and glaciers set against a cloudless blue sky. The men in this village were all armed with matchlocks which they used to shoot large numbers of ibex. These antiquated muskets, fired by means of a fuse, the hunters shot from a prone position using two prongs sticking out as a rest in front of the muzzle.

It was pleasant to be all collected together again; the night before I had felt like one of a scattered covey of partridges.

All night my feet burned like fire; they must have been slightly frost-bitten. The following day we marched for about three miles down the valley to Darkot, a rather attractive village in a small plain surrounded by mountains, some of them well above 20,000 feet. I spent most of the day outside the house we were in reading in the hot sun. The Rajah of Yasin arrived from the hot springs at Qasin Sheshma and in the evening I went out hawking with him; his hawks killed two sparrows.

Leaving Darkot early the next morning in fine, sunny weather we took it easy and stopped for the day at 1 PM at Barkulti. After a three-hour march from Barkulti we arrived at Yasin, a village of scattered farmsteads on rising ground between two streams. The Rajah of Yasin, Mahbub Ali Khan, lived in a large compound which from a distance looked like a fort. The compound, enclosed by a wall of rough stone, mud and wooden beams, was divided into several enclosures. All the buildings were in the local style and the larger buildings were decorated with some fine ibex heads. We stayed in the dak bungalow a little way up a side valley to the west of Yasin. The Rajah gave me a curry lunch at his house, where we sat in a large room with carved wooden pillars and the usual smoke-vent in the roof. It was all rather dilapidated.

Most of the Rajah's retainers carried a hawk on their fists; one had a kestrel. The Rajah had two or three peregrine falcons which were apparently still moulting; the peregrines were all kept in the same darkened room and not allowed out, but I was told they would be ready for hawking by November. The hawks had bells on their legs, and a hood which only half-obscured their sight. They were caught by a leather thong fastened round their necks, instead of jesses such as Arab falconers attach to the bird's legs. They told me that newly caught hawks have their eyes sewn up for two days. The locals did not appear to use lures but held out their fist and called. The hawk was only a short distance away in a tree or perched on a fence; when it alighted on the fist it was given a little meat.

Next morning it had turned cold and overcast, with clouds only 500–1,000 feet above us, smothering the view and bringing showers of drizzling rain at intervals. When we eventually halted to cook a meal, some rather surly villagers refused to give us any dry wood and we had to make do with tea brewed on a fire of damp shrubs.

We crossed the milky blue-green river by a suspension bridge opposite Gupis. The Rajah of Gupis, Hussain Ali Khan, made us welcome and gave us tea, biscuits and grapes; his son, a lieutenant in the Gilgit Scouts, was at home on leave and the Rajah of Punyial, Muhammad Anwar Khan, was there also. Afterwards we went down to the river to fish, using spoons and silver minnows, for trout. First introduced here in 1932, these trout were said to run up to 14 lbs; the Rajah of Gupis caught one weighing about half a pound. That night I dined at the Rajah's house, a small, unpretentious building, where some fifteen guests were assembled. During the evening a band played polo music to warn everyone that there was going to be polo on the morrow.

The polo match was played in the afternoon in a strong, very cold east wind. The field, which had stone walls on both sides, measured about 30 yards across by 250 yards in length. It occupied a pleasant site on a shelf above the river with ter-raced fields rising on the other side. The Rajah of Gupis and the Rajah of Punyial were both good players. They played with six a side and changed ends after each goal. The two chukkers each lasted about half an hour during which the band played at intervals. The first team to score nine goals was the winner. Among the spectators I noticed several Pathan types with turbans, probably from Tangir or Darel.

That evening after dinner, the Rajahs played a variety of local, Punjabi, Persian and Turkish melodies on the *rabab*, a sort of banjo, and three mandolins known as sitars. These instruments were of mulberry wood and very well made. The Rajah of Punyial, a gifted old man, was the most expert per-former. Of the four Rajahs I had met on this journey, I liked these two best, and Gupis best of all. During my stay at Gupis the rajah provided all our food and when we left he gave me a length of locally woven cloth for an overcoat.

I was violently sick all night. The next day's march of twenty-four miles, from Gupis to Gakuch, seemed a long way as I was feeling off-colour. Faiz had seen the local doctor in Gupis who cut the skin off his blisters and made a real mess of his feet. I had told Faiz to leave them alone. He now needed a horse to ride all the way from here to Gilgit.

Like yesterday, this was a cold, unpleasant day with a strong east wind which rose to a gale in the afternoon. The snow-capped mountains, rising practically sheer from the clear, bottle-green-coloured river, were obscured for most of the time by low cloud.

We arrived at 4 PM at Gakuch, which must have been a spectacular place in fine weather. I heard that the Rajah of Punyial had sent a message saying I was to be provided with chickens and whatever else I needed. A lot of tamarisk trees grew here in a wide valley surrounded by precipitous mountains topped with snow. The confluence, where the Gilgit river flowed in from Ishkoman, was about three miles upstream.

Two more days' easy marching brought us to Gilgit by the early afternoon. Almost six weeks had passed since Faiz Muhammad and I had set off on foot up the Kagan valley.

These final stages of my journey were pleasant but uneventful. The strong east wind had lost its bitter edge and dismal banks of low-lying cloud had given way to clear blue skies. Faiz's blistered feet were by now turning septic; when we stopped for the night at Gulapur I gave him an injection of penicillin and some Chloromycetin. This was all I could do for him until his feet were properly treated by a doctor in Peshawar.

While I was in Gilgit, Ali Riza Pahlawi, the Shah of Persia's brother, turned up at the end of his shooting trip in the Pamirs. He had got three Ovis poli in the Little Pamirs, besides two large brown bear and an ibex. That evening the Prince and I had a long talk about big-game hunting over dinner with Khan Muhammad Jan Khan, the political agent.

I was delayed in Gilgit for three days until the aeroplane, which had broken down, arrived and took us to Rawalpindi. From there I travelled by bus to Peshawar where I spent a week with John Dent before returning home to England.

While I was in Peshawar I drove with Mir Ajam, the political agent whom I had met the year before in Chitral, all round the head of an attractive valley along the Afghan frontier. On our way back to Peshawar the following morning we passed several small bands of Powindah nomads on the road with their donkeys, oxen and camels laden with timber. I felt that these Powindah must be one of the finest-looking races in the world.

HAZARAJAT

1954

AFTER SIX MONTHS in the Iraqi Marshes, living in semi-submerged houses and going about in a canoe, I was again anxious to stretch my legs on the mountaintops.

I had already seen the mountains of Nuristan from the villages of the Black Kafirs when I had visited Chitral in 1952. I resolved to go there but found that permission to enter that virtually unadministered region would be difficult to obtain.

When I arrived in Kabul in July 1954, I therefore asked instead for permission to travel in the Hazarajat. This I knew would be more easily forthcoming. I hoped by first travelling this region to establish my reputation in the eyes of the Afghan government so that another year they would give me a permit for Nuristan. The Hazarajat was in any case an interesting and little-known area and I was unaware of any European who had travelled there before me. This seemed strange since the Hazaras had been extensively recruited into the Indian Army. In 1903–4 the Indian government raised a battalion of Hazara Pioneers under Major C. W. Jacob from Hazara refugees who had crossed into British India from Central Afghanistan. The battalion was disbanded in 1933. They had served on the Frontier and in France and Mesopotamia during the First World War.

Despite this I had found out very little about the Hazaras,

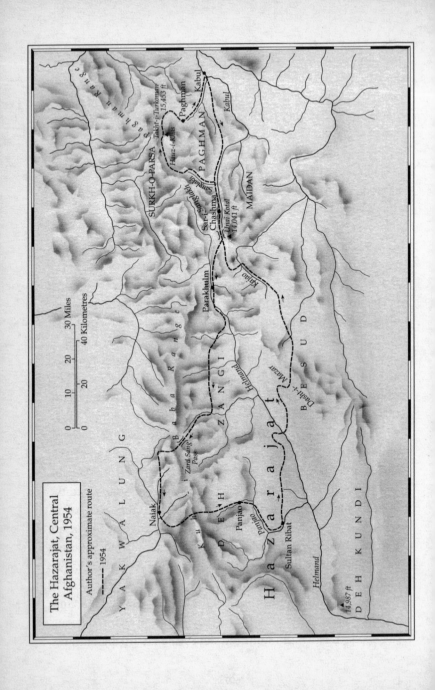

The Hazarajat, Central Afghanistan, 1954

Author's approximate route
------- 1954

and almost nothing more recent than a thirteen-page article devoted to them in the *Gazetteer of Afghanistan*, published in 1882. After travelling for six weeks among the Hazaras I realized that many of the statements in this article were either inaccurate or misleading.

The Hazaras are of Mongol descent and inhabit a large area in central Afghanistan. They were settled there in the thirteenth century either by Genghis Khan's son, Jagatai, or by his grandson, Mangu, in order to guard the marches after the Mongol invasion. It is unlikely that they originally all belonged to one tribe. More probably they were followers of chiefs selected for their loyalty from different tribes and races in the Mongol army. Even today most of the Hazaras are unmistakably Mongol in appearance, but they have abandoned the Mongol language and, with the possible exception of a few villages near Herat, they now speak an Iranian dialect composed largely of modern Iranian, some Mongol and another unidentified language. Estimates of their population varied but it seemed that Hazaras who belong to the Shiah sect of Islam numbered about a million.

I flew from Basra on 28 July to Karachi and went from there to Kabul, where I stayed with the British Ambassador, Sir David Lascelles, who obtained the necessary permission for my journey in the Hazarajat. The Afghan government provided me with an interpreter, thirty-four years old, called Jan Baz. I was fortunate to have him with me; although a townsman he endured the inevitable hardships without complaint, and during a journey of nearly 400 miles showed patience and tact in handling the Hazaras.

Starting from the Unai Kotal, at the head of the Maidan, and crossing the Helmand river near Parakhulm, we worked our way upwards along the southern slopes of Kuh-i-Baba until we crossed this 17,000-foot-high range by the Zard Sang Pass. We then visited Naiak, recrossed Kuh-i-Baba to Panjao, and followed the Panjao river down to Sultan Ribat; here we were forced eastwards by impassable gorges and had some difficulty in getting back over the Helmand. We climbed up through some very broken country to the northern edge of the Dasht-i-Mazar, in Besud, which we skirted before descending the broad and fertile valley of the Kajao, to Kharbet. From there we went to Unai Kotal, down to Sar-i-Chashma and up the Sanglakh valley. We then crossed the steep mountain range on the north side of the valley into Surkh-o-Parsa, recrossed this mountain range to the north of Takht-i-Turkoman, and descended from the holy pools of Hauz-i-Khas to Paghman and Kabul. During the six weeks Jan Baz and I travelled in the Hazarajat, of its four districts, Deh Kundi, Deh Zangi, Besud and Yakwalung, Deh Kundi was the only one I did not enter.

On 10 August Jan Baz and I travelled from Kabul by Land Rover to Qalat-i-Wazir, just short of the Unai Kotal, where we spent the night in a roadside serai. The following morning we set off on foot accompanied by a Sayid, Muhammad Ali Agha, and two donkeys, which we later exchanged for a pony, loaded with our kit, towards Kuh-i-Baba at the heart of the Hazarajat. I could see patches of snow on this range of bare, tawny mountains ahead of us; running from east to west for eighty miles, 15,000–17,000 feet high, they formed the western extremity of the Hindu Kush.

On 12 August we left Jaukol where we had spent the night in a large, fort-like serai and made our way down the Helmand valley as far as Parakhulm. Crops of wheat, beans, peas and some potatoes grew beside the small scattered villages in the valley. At Qala Nau (New Fort), the owner, a friendly Kizilbash,

gave us green tea, bread and eggs for lunch in a large, bare, carpeted room decorated with attractive incised plaster-work. The
Kizilbash's servants were Hazaras. I was to learn by experience
that theft among the Hazaras was very rare and universally
detested; the Hazaras just did not steal and consequently were
much in demand as servants in Kabul and elsewhere.

Parakhulm, further down the valley, consisted merely of a
few tea-shops and a rather dilapidated fort manned by an
Afghan official and some soldiers. The official was away when
we arrived but his clerk gave us permission to spend the night
in a very bug-ridden shai khana, where the bugs came pouring
out of the walls even in daylight. We chose instead to sleep on
the verandah. When we tried to buy a chicken they asked three
times the going rate so for dinner we had bread and scrambled
eggs. In the evening some men from the Maidan sang songs
accompanied by a mandolin.

The next day we continued on down the road for about three
miles and then followed the river to the village of Panj Ausia
(the Five Mills) where a tall, distinguished-looking Hazara
brought us a meal of bread and eggs. From here we kept to the
river bank or else along the bare, stony hillsides. We passed
villages; clusters of primitive houses built with stones and mud,
wherever there was a spring or a stream. The hillsides were
cultivated with wheat, beans, peas and clover; poplars often
grew near the houses.

Some hours before sunset we camped for the night at
Darun-i-Jui inside the walls of a half-built house. The men
were all out in the fields, except one who seemed unforthcom-
ing. In contrast to Chitral and Hunza, whenever the villagers in
these parts saw us they would bolt, imagining we were government officials. The children too were nervous and suspicious;

looking at me they would cry, 'He will hit us', but I would soon win their confidence by giving them some sugar and letting them play with my torch. The men at Darun-i-Jui relaxed when they saw we were not requisitioning eggs and chickens. We gave them endless cups of tea while I tried to converse with one of them, a mullah, who spoke bad Arabic.

We left early on 14 August and followed the river, with the long, jagged outline of snow-streaked Kuh-i-Baba on our right. Due to a shortage of wood, many of the village houses we passed had domed roofs of rough stones; several had been built under a single, shared roof, on top of which lay great heaps of dry cow-dung and artemisia for winter fuel. A small boy had accompanied us for part of the way; we pressed him to share a meal with us at Pul-i-Afghan, where we stopped in the gateway of a large, well-built house. After lunch the boy went on his way, but we found him again, with an elderly Haji, at the roadside beyond a big tumbledown Kizilbash fort, waiting to invite us to their village.

With them we crossed the Helmand river and climbed up to a small village known as Aklil Murda. All the houses shared a communal roof; the interiors were like dungeons, with tiny windows high up on the walls and in the centre of the roof an outlet for smoke. That night we slept on a flat roof between the domes, under a cold clear sky; we always avoided sleeping in their rooms, because of the bugs, unless the cold was intense.

We were off again by seven the next day. We crossed the river and continued downstream as far as Tagob where we found the villagers hard at work making cloth. The Hazarajat is famous throughout Afghanistan for its ghee and a cloth called *barak*.

Women weave this cloth out of doors on looms, and the men soften it by placing it on a flat stone over a fire and then stamping on it for a whole day while they keep it continuously damp. They weave rugs but do not treat them over a fire, and they also make felt floor coverings on which they sit or sleep.

At Tagob I took some photographs of a good-looking old man and his son; after a meal, we climbed steadily up a succession of small valleys, planted with wheat and clover, which divided the steep hillsides above the river. The going here was easy and the country was agreeably spacious. Despite a general impression of emptiness, we saw many small villages flanked by poplars tucked away in the valley depths below the bare, stony hillsides. Apart from a few willows and tamarisks along the Helmand, these poplars were the only trees I saw anywhere on Kuh-i-Baba. The air on the mountainsides, indeed in the whole country, was scented with artemisia.

That night we stayed at Jan Karra, a newly built village where everyone gave us a very friendly welcome. I took a lot of photographs of the villagers including some whose features looked less Mongolian than those of most Hazaras.

Next morning two boys helped us to carry our bags of rice-flour to the top of a very steep hill between Jan Karra and the next valley. From here on the valleys grew steeper-sided and deeper than before. As soon as we got down to Hoskau on the valley floor we stopped and bought a kid; Jan Baz cooked a good lunch of soup and fried goat's liver which we ate under a willow by a stream.

We had to cross two more ridges before we reached Shar-i-Jalil, in a steep side-valley about two and a half hours' march from Hoskau, where we camped for the night on a small roof.

Both sides of Kuh-i-Baba, I discovered, were seamed with a

succession of valleys like those we had encountered between Jan Karra and Shar-i-Jalil. Although these valleys were usually steep I noticed few rocky outcrops; their sides were mostly earth and scree covered with thistles, coarse grass, hogweed, rhubarb and cushion plants. The villagers broke up thistles for fodder, by treading them out with oxen. On the way to Shar-i-Jalil all the hillsides were covered with crops of *lalma*, rain-grown wheat which gives a better grain but a much lower yield than *gandum*, the irrigated wheat grown on good ground near the villages. During my journey in the Hazarajat, besides wheat, the villagers were harvesting crops of peas and broad beans. Few of them grew other vegetables such as turnips, marrows or onions, and nowhere in the areas I visited did I see fruit trees. When I asked them why they did not grow fruit, the villagers usually replied, 'It is not our custom'; but at Shar-i-Jalil they said it was impossible because of the heavy winter snow and intense cold.

Here also, in winter, I heard that wolves grew very bold and frequently attacked the villagers' flocks of sheep and goats. I was constantly surprised that such large communities could survive throughout the winter at altitudes of 8,000–12,000 feet under these harsh conditions. Snow usually started to fall in November and soon made travel outside the villages almost impossible. The Hazaras sometimes travelled on crude snow-shoes, about a foot in diameter and circular in shape, which they made from twisted willow saplings, with two crossbars but without any netting, but most of them remained in their villages until the spring.

During summer and autumn the villagers spent every spare moment collecting fuel and forage from the mountains to tide them through the long winter months. Not only were there no trees here but no scrub and no bushes. Their fuel consisted of dried dung and various plants such as artemisia; such fuel is adequate, even if unsatisfactory, for cooking purposes, but it can be of little value in warming a house unless burned in quantities which would be quite unprocurable. It was surprising, too, to find so little soil erosion in these mountains where practically every kind of plant that grows was either grubbed up for fuel or cut for fodder.

On our way up the steep, narrow valley from Shar-i-Jalil we picked up a man to help us carry our loads over the pass and down to Katahokh, a large, picturesque village with a fort and a watch-tower at the junction of two valleys.

While we were at Katahokh two Kuchis arrived with camels loaded with grain to be ground at the local mill. Later the Kuchi who was herding the camels allowed one of them to stray into a field of wheat and the Hazara farmer who owned the field drove out the camel and gave the Kuchi herdsman a severe thrashing with a heavy stick. The Kuchi never lifted a hand in self-defence, though he protested volubly. Here was an example of the friction which always arises whenever nomads and cultivators meet; the age-old conflict between the Desert and the Sown.

In the Hazarajat large numbers of nomad Pathans from the Ahmadzai, Mohmand and Safi tribes travelled up the valleys in the early summer to their grazing grounds on the mountaintops and returned again in the autumn on their way down to Pakistan. These nomad Pathans were known by various names: in Pakistan as Powindah, in Afghanistan generally as Kuchis, but to the Hazaras as Afghans, and in the far north as Kandaris. They had with them great numbers of camels, and large herds of sheep and goats. These Kuchis brought cloth, sugar, tea and other goods which they traded with the Hazaras for grain and flour. To this extent the Kuchis and Hazaras were dependent on one another, but the Kuchis despised the Hazaras and the Hazaras, like the farmer at Katahokh, were obviously in no way overawed by these swashbuckling Pathans whom they detested.

At the far end of a narrow, rocky gorge crowned with pinnacles of rock, we met other nomads, Uthman Khel from the Mohmand tribe, who were moving down from the highland pastures. As they were just about to make camp they asked us to stop with them. There were about a dozen tents, which the women pitched, each divided into two compartments by baggage. All of us, men, women and children, sat together in the larger area of one tent where the women cooked and drank tea with the men.

These Kuchis were an attractive, good-looking crowd, full of life, far more colourful and more fun to be with than the generally tight-fisted, stolid Hazaras who, despite their hardihood, toughness and honesty, I found rather dreary. Some Hazaras we encountered were more forthcoming and hospitable than others, but such characteristics did vary, perhaps as a result of their mixed tribal and racial ancestry. The Kuchi women did not veil, wore colourful, embroidered baggy red trousers and were not in the least shy. The Hazara women did not veil either and compared to the men's drab, unbecoming, usually ragged apparel, their clothes were always bright. The Hazara women's head-dress varied in style according to the locality and was often decorated with innumerable coins; most of their clothes were red in colour. The Hazara men wore a long cotton shirt, trousers, a coat, sometimes a waistcoat, and over everything a cloak or top-coat. They all wore skull caps and generally a white turban tied so that one end fell down over the shoulder. At Surkh-o-Parsa a few men and boys wore knitted and woollen caps with tassels and elsewhere some old men wore lambskin caps which until recently, I was told, had been the common Hazara male head-dress.

I found the Hazara women modest and even shy; I disagreed entirely with the view expressed in the *Gazetteer of Afghanistan* that 'The character of their women for unblushing immorality also appears to be universal; they are handsome and engaging and the opportunities offered, to strangers even, by some tribes are said to be shameless.' It may be said that the women were not very chaste, but the custom of *kuri bistan*, which consists of lending wives to strangers for a night or a week, was almost certainly a fabrication. I never came across it.

The Kuchis had come a longish way, about twelve miles I gathered, starting in the middle of the night. They said they were going down to Jalalabad and the Khyber. Their flocks of sheep and goats, guarded by some magnificent dogs, grazed slowly along the hilltops. They spent about five months every year in the Hazarajat and five months near Jalalabad; each of these journeys to and from the mountains took a month.

From the Kuchis' encampment we went up the valley, past the ruins of a long-abandoned village, over a fairly steep pass. The hillsides all around were covered with coarse green grass; from the wild, high country at the top of the pass, a way led up over the summit of Kuh-i-Baba, northwards to Bamian. After a sharp descent to Kajak, a small scattered village among bright-green fields of unripe wheat, we spent a cold night camped on the roof of an empty house.

It stayed very cold next morning until the sun was up, with a chill west wind blowing along the valley. On our way down the valley we passed some Ahmadzai tents and, further on, more of these nomads coming down off the high pastures. There were only women at the Ahmadzai encampment; the men were out on the mountains with their sheep and camels.

It seemed to me nonsense to call the Hazaras badly off. Every available inch of ground in these valleys was under some form of cultivation, including excellent crops of wheat, barley, beans, peas and clover. Apart from cereals and vegetables the Hazaras also kept flocks of sheep and goats, beside herds of small, black, humped cattle, which provided them with butter, curds and milk. Before this I had supposed that the Hazarajat was a desperately poor country and, indeed, my first view from the slopes of Kuh-i-Baba confirmed this impression. I had looked out across the succession of deep valleys and over bare, stony, rolling hillsides parched and tawny-coloured. In this landscape the few patches of green cultivation were especially noticeable. But I now realized that this impression of barrenness and poverty, although very natural, was a totally false one, due to the configuration of the ground. As I wandered through this country I discovered that almost every fold and wrinkle in the ground to which water could be conducted was cultivated. There were many springs, especially on the southern slopes of Kuh-i-Baba, and streams in all the valleys. As I walked up these valleys it often seemed that the cultivation would peter out round the next corner, and yet it would go on, sometimes widening out and sometimes narrowing, until eventually we came to the high valleys where all cultivation ceased. All ploughing was done with oxen, even on the steepest hillsides, like those above Kajak and Ghawas, where it was difficult to imagine how this had been achieved.

On 20 August we left Said Kul Kushta an hour after sunrise and walked up the valley past fields of barley, clover and harvested wheat. Then we followed, or rather waded along a stream flowing through a very confined, rocky, limestone gorge below jagged peaks where lammergeyers and ravens wheeled in the wind-torn sky above us. Here for the first time on this journey we found ourselves among the real mountains.

At a nomad encampment beyond the gorge the owner, an Essa Khel from the Ahmadzai, produced tea but refused to give us anything else. A mile or two further on, however, we encountered more hospitable Essa Khel who gave us bread and tea; they invited us to stop with them for the night which we did, camped inside a circular stone wall which these nomads used as their mosque.

The Essa Khel, I was told, wintered close to the Russian frontier near Mazar-i-Sharif; as a tax, levied by the Afghan administration, they carried part of the government's share of the Hazara wheat crop to Kabul. There were few men at the tents; the rest were camped with their grazing camels and flocks of sheep and goats higher up on the mountains. The Essa Khel said there were a great many ibex on the cliffs round here, and also brown bear.

A bitterly cold, strong north wind was blowing as we made our way up the valley next morning towards the Zard Sang, or Yellow Rock, Pass which the locals call Sar-i-Bulak. We climbed by a steep track, past more nomad tents in a side-valley, but took a wrong turning near the pass and had to work back along the top to join the other track. This unforeseen detour gave me a good view, despite rather hazy conditions, back the way we had come. From the top of the Zard Sang Pass the country to the north looked much flatter, with no obvious peaks or mountain ranges. Apart from some sheer-sided gorges, it appeared generally undulating and dry; Kuh-i-Baba fell away rapidly to these downs with no intervening foothills.

As we descended by easy stages from the pass, I saw that this side of the mountain was indeed much drier; consequently the vegetation changed and I now saw several plants I had not seen on Kuh-i-Baba's south side. Unlike my previous journeys in Swat, Chitral and Hunza, on this one I collected all the plants I saw in fruit or flower; my collection, which eventually numbered over two hundred specimens, is now in the British Natural History Museum and includes cereals and vegetables grown by the Hazaras. The number of plants found in the autumn was bound to be limited but they proved to be of considerable interest.

Below the Zard Sang, we found half a dozen Mohmand tents close to a sheer-sided mass of pale rock overhanging the stream. We stopped here and rested ourselves and our laden pony before continuing on down the valley to Barlay Riq where we camped. The Hazaras in two villages we passed were all busy collecting winter fuel and forage off the mountainsides. The men carried bundles of rhubarb leaves, thistles and wild hogweed either on their backs or loaded on donkeys; there were no mules in this country and the Hazaras did not own camels, since it is too cold here for them in winter. All the camels I saw in the Hazarajat belonged to the Kuchis. Even now, at the end of August, it was freezing hard at night on the northern slopes of Kuh-i-Baba and the cows, sheep and goats were taken inside the houses. Four or five cows and some sixty sheep and goats would thrust their way through the narrow doorway and disappear down a dark passage into the bowels of the house.

We halted briefly in the second village at a house owned by a Karbalawi, the name given to any man who has made the pilgrimage to the Holy City of Karbala, in southern Iraq; Karbala, the burial place of the Shiah martyr, Husain, and the Holy City

Above: A man who helped us at Spanj, where we changed our ponies for yaks.

Below: A Turis boy at Kurram.

Above: Old man at Karumbar.

Below: Hazara man at Unai Kotal in the Maidan, where I began my journey.

Above: Tagob, a typical Hazara mountain village in Deh Zangi. The house roofs are domed in those areas where the villagers are short of timber for beams.

Below: The Sayid from the Maidan on top of the Zard Sang Pass with his pony which carried our kit.

Left: We passed this old man on our way along the Panjao river valley in Deh Zangi.

Above: A Kuchi of the Ahmadzai. These Kuchis camp in summer on the mountain tops.

Left: Lakan Khel in the Dara valley.

Above: Mohmand Kuchis camped near Jangal Murda.

Below: Mia Khel Sayids carrying bundles of lucerne down to Jalalabad from Besud.

Above: Saiydon in the Maidan. The family of the
Sunni Sayid who accompanied me with his pony.

Below: The Koli Barit valley in Surkh-o-Parsa.

Above: A stone building resembling a monastery, in the Colom Bela valley, Surkh-o-Parsa.

Below: In Besud, north of the Helmand, a Hazara village with Kuh-i-Baba in the background.

Above: Kabul.

Right: Tajiks.

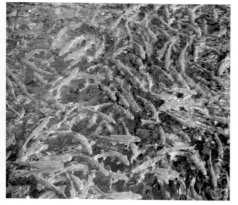

Left: Sacred fish in the pools at
Sar-i-Chashma by the source
of the Kabul river, at the head
of the Maidan valley.

Above: Tajik shepherds in the Panjshir valley.

Below: Nuristanis from Kulam whom we met in the Chamar valley.

Above: Near the
source of the East
Chamar river in
Nuristan.

Right: Tajik villager
carrying an
instrument used for
stranding cotton.

Overleaf: The top of
the Chamar valley.

Left: Nuristani boys at Mangur in the Ramgul valley.

Below: A boy at Kulam, wearing a typical Nuristani woollen cap.

Below: Nuristani children at Puchal.

Right: Puchal in the Ramgul valley, Nuristani villager sitting on a chair backed with ibex horns.

Above: In the Linar valley.

Below: Gujurs from Kantiwar who joined us in the Wanasgul valley.

Previous page: Above Shahi, in the Alingar
valley, Laghman.

Above: Near Sar-i-Sang, the only place where
for centuries lapis lazuli has been mined.

of Najaf, built round the tomb of Husain's father, the Caliph Ali, became the goal of pilgrims from across the world. However, I was interested to find here that a visit to Meshed al Ridha in north-eastern Iran conferred no title and little distinction, whereas among the Shiah tribes of southern Iraq a visit to Meshed entitled the pilgrim to call himself Zair, a much coveted distinction.

The Karbalawi owned a large number of sheep and goats and was evidently prosperous, yet like other Hazaras he could not have been more inhospitable and provided us with nothing.

So it was throughout our journey. Nearly always, when we arrived at a village and prepared to stop, someone would come forward and suggest that we should find very much better quarters in some other village a mile or two further on. This was an unusual failing among Muslims. The Hazaras were never unfriendly, just mean and unwelcoming. I found the Shiah Sayids in the Hazarajat as inhospitable as the tribesmen, whereas towards the end of our journey when we travelled in the Maidan and in the Sanlakh valley, among Sunni Sayids and Tajiks, we met with a very different welcome. Time and again these villagers pressed me to stop and drink tea, and towards evening many people working in the fields shouted out to us as we passed, inviting us to spend the night with them.

After a bitterly cold night at Barlay Riq I woke to find my cup of water frozen over, a chilling reminder of freezing autumn nights in Hunza the previous year.

On the featureless, dry, dusty downs below Kuh-i-Baba we came upon several Hazara summer camps. In these *ailoqs*, or *khirqa* as they were known locally, the Hazaras lived in primitive, circular stone shelters roofed with a framework of poles inclining inwards and upwards to a point and overlaid with some shrubs. A few mats were sometimes thrown over these poles to give rather more shelter from the sun. Later, in Surkh-o-Parsa, I saw a few small, primitive, yurt-like dwellings, made of mats fastened over a framework of willow saplings.

At one of the ailoqs, inhabited by Sayids, they and Hazaras from neighbouring camps and villages had gathered in considerable numbers to celebrate a wedding. The main features of the day's entertainment were rifle-shooting, and two horse-races for which the assembled crowds could only produce five horses. The Hazaras said that their chief amusements were horse-racing and shooting at a target from the saddle while at the gallop. But while the *Gazetteer of Afghanistan* (1882) estimated the Hazara cavalry in tens of thousands, I only saw a dozen horses during my journey. There was no dancing or music at the wedding since, much to my surprise, these people, who spend six months a year cooped up in their snowbound villages, neither danced nor played any musical instruments. The Hazaras were, however, fond of poetry and I was assured that some of their poetry was really good.

After lunch everyone dispersed. We walked on, beneath a cloudless sky, down to the floor of the valley where the parched downland suddenly gave way to green patches of cultivation. On the road through the valley we were hailed by an enormously fat, cheerful-looking fellow smothered in weapons, riding on a donkey. His name was Mir; the second son of the Sayid chief of Yakwalung, Shah Mirza Hussain Agha, he was on his way up to the family's summer encampment. We stopped for the night at their fort where I met the Sayid, a blind old man, and Mir's elder and younger brothers. The Sayid's fourth son, the present *arbob* in this district, was away.

For dinner they gave us an inadequate amount of bread soaked in thin soup and half a chicken between Jan Baz, our

Sayid ponyman and myself, thus disappointing my hopes of a good meal.

The following morning, after breakfast, we carried on downstream to Naiak, a small place with a fine view down the valley to some mountains flecked with snow. On either side of the valley the sandstone slopes, covered with purplish-red earth, appeared very much eroded. Apart from a large, mud-built fort, which housed the acting governor, Naiak consisted of little more than a handful of shops. The acting governor was quite friendly, put us up in a small office and gave us some fish – barbel I think and not bad – for dinner. I spent the time at Naiak sorting through my collection of plants and writing up my diary.

Starting at 7.30 AM we kept to the Panjao road, except for about an hour and a half when we followed a track over some higher ground. I collected a surprising number of plants, including several species of salt bush. The country beyond Naiak, however, even the mountaintops, struck me as unimpressive. Apart from seeing a peregrine falcon chasing a rock-pigeon, nothing else occurred during our five hours' walk to Sausnau, where we slept inside a newly built house. The valley here was more attractive and the villagers took a lot of trouble finding a chicken for our dinner.

It remained very cold next morning until we got into the sun some way along the road from Sausnau. Where the cultivations ended, a track led over the ugly green and purple mountainside, threading among stones and prickly vegetation, to the Shatu Pass. On the far side of the pass lay a more attractive country with open views over distant mountain ranges. We passed three youngsters herding their camels before we arrived at a Pathan encampment belonging to some Ala-el-din of the Ahmadzai.

While we rested here I took a number of photographs of two very good-looking lads, using a 90mm portrait lens. It was only after I went to the Marshes of southern Iraq that I acquired any additional lenses for my camera, a Leica II which I had bought in 1934. Previously all my photographs had been taken with this camera and its standard 50mm lens.

We left at 3 PM and marched along a broad upland valley past more Ala-el-din camped beside their grazing flocks, until we reached Kotal Chal, a gorge reputed to harbour some warm springs; everywhere I looked, water oozed out from the limestone cliffs and the air smelt faintly of sulphur. The steep mountainsides nearby were scored by long chutes down which the villagers propelled their heavy bundles of fuel, collected on the high tops, to the valley. Below us lay several small Hazara villages and fields; at one of these villages, called Dehbarak, we camped for the night on the flat roof of a Karbalawi's house.

We hung on at Dehbarak, until the sun was on our roof and I had shaved, before setting off down the valley. After about two miles, we caught up with groups of Pathans and their flocks, some moving along the road, others on the scree-covered hillsides. From time to time stones dislodged by these flocks bombarded the track in large numbers.

Shortly before midday we arrived at Panjao (the Five Streams) where a considerable crowd had gathered in the gaily-decorated bazaar to celebrate Independence Day. This was the third day of these Jaishan celebrations. Jan Baz went to the fort, where Afghan dances were being performed in the enclosure, and told the governor of our arrival; the governor sent the police commandant to take us down to the guest-house and here we waited for three hours before we were given a very poor meal.

In the evening some Kuchis danced to a pipe, and drums which they tapped with sticks; this involved much tossing about of the dancers' hair, bobbed in the distinctive Khutwak manner.

When we left Panjao next morning the police commandant sent one of his policemen with us. There had been trouble between the Hazaras and Kuchis in Sia Darachiu, the main Panjao valley, and the commandant feared that either of them might do something to harm us and then blame it on the other. The policeman would consequently remain with us for three days until we reached the Sirkjui valley beyond Sultan Ribat.

At Muhak, on the way to Sultan Ribat, we halted at a fair-sized fort, with an orchard of apricots and mulberry trees, owned by a middle-aged Hazara.

The Sayids in Doni Waras, the next village, were a bloody crowd and inhospitable in the extreme even by local standards. Seeing that we intended to spend the night there, they urged us to go on down the valley and stay with the arbob; then, when we tried to buy a chicken they made difficulties even though they had plenty. In the end a party of nomads camped nearby, Bahram Khel from the Logar, provided us with some bread. I thought, 'Give me Kuchis every time.'

Quite a considerable stream flowed along the Panjao valley among scenery pleasingly varied by stands of poplar and many willows. After marching for two or three hours, we halted for a meal at Sultan Ribat, a small village with a fort, where some Bahram Khel were camped on the opposite bank.

We then continued up the smaller, more wooded Patu valley

which joined the Panjao valley from the east. Here again, like the Shatu Pass, I noticed how the ugly purplish-red colour of the hills clashed with the yellow-green fields of rape and *turbak*, plants from which the Hazaras extracted oil for their lamps. We stopped for the night at a fort owned by the arbob, Ramadhan Ali Khan Karbalawi, a youngish man who lived here with three of his brothers. The fort was well positioned, high up on a steep-sided spur, with a clear view of the pass leading to the Sirkjui valley.

The arbob and his family, whom I liked, put us up in a well-kept, comfortable guest-room. A Sayid who spoke some Arabic was also stopping here, and the Sayid's disciple, a Hazara boy aged about fifteen. The boy had sores on his thigh, which I doctored. In doing so I noticed that he was uncircumcised, which was unusual since most Hazara boys were circumcised when they were about six years old; this was done in autumn after the crops had been harvested. This boy prayed assiduously and remained with his head touching the ground for as long as ten minutes at a time. Neither Jan Baz nor I had ever seen anyone pray like this.

Next morning we set off at eight from the arbob's fort and crossed the pass into the Sirkjui valley. From the top of the pass we sent our police escort back to Panjao. The Sirkjui valley was steep-sided and narrower than either the Panjao or Patu valleys, with some villages and cultivation including tobacco, the first I had seen in the Hazarajat. Here, as in a few other places, the villagers grew tobacco for chewing or for smoking in hubble-bubbles, but none of them smoked cigarettes.

For the past ten days or more the skies had been cloudless. We took advantage of the fine weather, loitering at Chijin by some tall, shady willows until the middle of the afternoon; then we went on down the valley to a large arbob fort owned by Zamin Ali Khan, the elder brother of our host of the previous night, Ramadhan Ali Khan. Since the cattle, sheep and goats were all driven into the fort at night, we camped beside a pool just outside its rectangular enclosure, and later the arbob's family gave us a good dinner.

We were strongly advised not to proceed any further down the Sirkjui valley than Shina Ribat, where we halted for a meal at noon the following day. From here the track deteriorated badly, and we were now forced eastward to avoid impassable gorges which prevented us from following directly up the Helmand river. Instead we went up a narrow side-valley past some Kuchi tents, then villages and wheatfields, to the top of the short, fairly steep pass; here, at Batkol, we spent the night with an obliging old man and his family. That evening I killed a large red spider, a beastly looking animal; these spiders were said to be more poisonous than scorpions, but I thought this unlikely.

On 1 September we left Batkol at 8 A M, after I had done some doctoring, and made our way down a small, steeply sloping valley. I began to feel rather doubtful if we should get down one particularly steep, bare incline where we had to make a track. But after two and a half hours we arrived down by the Helmand where it was shut in by a gorge. We had to ford the river at this point, thigh-deep in pretty cold water, as it was impossible to get up- or down-stream on our side.

After a refreshing bathe and some tea, I set off again with Jan Baz and our Sayid up a steep hillside, over another pass, into Gunbadak, an attractive valley with a clear view back to the mountains beyond the Helmand river.

This was the third day of Muharram, which commemorates

the martyrdom of the Prophet's grandson, Husain, and we passed a house where some villagers were holding a prayer-meeting. Except for winter, when they slaughtered and dried the meat of any surplus livestock, the Hazaras seldom ate meat. However, meat was eaten on certain days during the month of Muharram. Then tens of thousands of sheep and goats were slaughtered throughout the Hazarajat, and their meat consumed at the mosques where everyone in the neighbourhood assembled to hear sacred readings from the Koran; women attending were confined to a separate room away from the men. In one small valley, I was told, no fewer than twelve sheep would be killed every day during Muharram. Almost no-one remained at home on these occasions, leaving their houses locked up and villages deserted.

The way from the fort, where we had spent the night, led up a steep mountainside, over a high pass, then descended sharply down into Sia Kol, the Black Valley, whose name presumably derived from the abundant granite and black igneous rocks that formed it. From the top of the pass we had an impressive view over another tributary of the Helmand river and the black mountains behind it. But the sight of these steep-sided mountains still ahead of us rather depressed Jan Baz.

Three side-valleys, one of which offered a likely route, ran down into Sia Kol from the east.

Coming along the lush, green valley floor I found several new plants, including a species of fern, growing among the rocks. We halted under some trees beside a pool above the only village, where the people fed us with mutton from a sheep which they had killed for Muharram.

We set off shortly after 2 in the afternoon, bearing east, up one of the three side-valleys where the cultivations extended for a considerable distance. A stiff climb up to the 10,000-foot-high pass at the head of this valley, followed by a steep descent, brought us after four hours to the valley of Gauhar Kol. By now it was getting dark. We camped under some willows outside the first house we came to where the owner, who was little more than a boy, and several other lads proved to be friendly and helpful. Crossing these two passes had made a long, tiring day, especially for the Sayid's pony.

Next morning we continued east over a small, bare hill, covered with coarse grass and thistles, into the Khar Kol valley. We stopped after two hours at a village mosque or prayer room, which was hung with banners and flagellation chains used by penitents in the Muharram procession. The villagers, a cheerful, pleasant crowd, gave us some meat from the Muharram sacrifices. One boy had a badly swollen knee and sores on his legs; I injected him with penicillin but feared he might have tuberculosis.

From Khar Kol we crossed into another valley, down a hillside strewn with boulders and great slabs of granite, then along the valley floor past fields of wheat and barley to Sari Top. Towards nightfall, the inhabitants of Sari Top returned from a prayer-meeting at another village across the valley, and provided us with meat for dinner.

Marching east from Khar Kol we climbed up through some very broken country to the northern edge of the Dasht-i-Mazar, a rolling downland 9,000 feet above sea-level with some rocky hills rising out of it. Apart from the springy green turf carpeting its hollows, which made walking very pleasant, the Dasht-i-Mazar was parched terrain; at Khairkhana, a small village in the Khawat valley where we fed and rested for three hours, they were desperately short of water.

The Kajao valley over the low watershed beyond Khawat was, by contrast, rich and fertile, irrigated by a sluggish, weed-filled stream. At one place, lower down this valley, we found the close-cropped turf underfoot actually submerged in water. Here in a spacious, attractive setting, with open views of the mountains ahead of us, I was struck by the varied colouring of hills, limestone rocks and fields – purple-greys, blues, off-white, yellow, orange and pale-green – softened by the hazy afternoon light.

We passed Qalat Hajdar, Fort of the Dragon, whose name derived from a fable that, here, a dragon had once been turned into stone. The fort stood at the head of the Kajao valley and not the Khawat as shown on the map which seemed to bear little relation to the ground. Most of the place names were unfamiliar to the average Hazara, who knew nothing about tribal divisions and very little about the country beyond his immediate neighbourhood.

The village houses in the Kajao valley, like those elsewhere in the Hazarajat, built of local stone and earth, inevitably took on the colour of their surroundings. In Kajao the villages, like the rocks and soil, were coloured a purplish-red. Shortly before sunset we arrived at Qalat Wakil, the arbob's house. The arbob and a Sayid who was with him appeared pretty offhand, until they discovered who I was, when they became offensive. The arbob had been at Markaz when the governor of Kabul had rung up and said that I was to be properly looked after. Their behaviour was typically Hazara, a sorry contrast with even the worst Arabs for hospitality. The carcass of a very dead donkey near the arbob's house smelt unpleasantly.

Next morning, we passed a deserted stretch of the valley where there were some wheatfields but no trees, and only occasional houses lying in ruins. Here we saw a party of Kuchis with their flocks, crossing the river.

Towards midday we stopped at Qala-i-Tahsildar, a well-constructed fort owned by the tahsildar, or tax-collector, of the district. The *tahsildar*, Muhammad Muhsin, was away at a prayer-meeting. No-one was in the fort, except for some small children, and we waited under some big poplars shading a pond.

Muhammad Muhsin proved to be elderly, extremely hospitable and welcoming. In the evening he produced horses for Jan Baz and myself. We went for a ride into the hills across the river to the south, where I managed to take some photographs of women at an encampment of Sultan Khel Ahmadzai. When we returned at sunset, Muhammad Muhsin gave us a really good dinner, the only decent meal I had been offered until then in the Hazarajat.

Although fuel was difficult to come by, the tahsildar's house had central heating ducts under the floors by means of which warm air from a fire was distributed to the various rooms.

The valley here was rich and fertile, wooded with poplars and cultivated with well-tended fields of wheat, beans, peas and lucerne. By the time we left at 7.15 A M everyone was out in the fields, harvesting, treading out the barley and peas with oxen, and winnowing. The Kajao river, which had barbel in it, reminded me of an English trout stream.

After marching down the valley for a couple of hours we stopped at a tea-shop in Dahani Garmau. Everything here was very expensive. The whole village gathered round to stare. I eventually got sick of this and felt relieved to be on our way again down the valley, and then up a track into the mountains. The steady climb up out of the valley led over a bare, rocky hillside, but was nowhere difficult. Shortly after 4 P M we topped a small rise and arrived at Uliat, a village with a fort and some cultivations, where we camped for the night. It had been another fine day with only a little cloud, the first cloud we had seen for almost three weeks.

The following morning we climbed over a tumbled mass of weathered granite boulders to the low pass above Uliat and, from there, to a high upland valley. Beyond the pass we met a party of Mia Khel Pushtu Sayids with twenty camels, carrying great bundles of lucerne to Jalalabad for their flocks. I took several photographs of these people who, compared with other Kuchis, struck me as an unprepossessing lot.

At Saukhtar, at the head of a tributary of the Kajao river, the villagers gave us two legs of mutton for lunch. Here, as elsewhere in the Hazarajat during Muharram, people from the widely scattered farmsteads assembled for prayer-meetings at lunchtime and then dispersed to their homes in the late afternoon. In most Shiah communities these sacred readings took place in the evenings after dinner.

Leaving Saukhtar, we kept to the edge of the Unai Kotal mountain, its steep, rocky flanks chequered with sunlight and slow-moving shadows cast by the clouds. After the next village, Yurt, we rejoined the Helmand river and followed this for some distance through a gorge of volcanic rock, until we eventually reached Qalat-i-Sayid. Coming along this stretch of the Helmand, between sixty-foot-high cliffs, we were twice forced across the river which was fortunately shallow and not very cold. Everyone agreed, however, that the way from here up the Helmand to its source was too steep and difficult; the pony was getting tired, and we therefore decided to go round by Sar-i-Chashma and the Sanglakh valley.

*

The Sayids at Qalat-i-Sayid were neither helpful nor hospitable. Thinking we might fare better among the Safi Kuchis, some of whom we heard were camped in the mountains nearby, we set off early to look for them. The Safis had already moved on, however, except for one tent where there were only women. An easy track brought us to the top of the Barbogha Pass; from here, we descended by a steeper built-up track to Barbogha, a Tajik village with a few Hazaras living in it and a camp of Mohmands who owned some of the fields.

The Tajiks at Barbogha proved to be helpful and obliging. We lunched there, and then carried on down the valley, past hillsides covered with bushes quite different from any I had seen in the Hazara country. All morning the weather had been fine and sunny but in the afternoon the sky grew overcast, and a few drops of rain began to fall as we neared Sar-i-Chashma.

Ali Ahmed Khan owned the fort at Sar-i-Chashma. His father, Sayid Ahmed, had been banished to Baghlan; a famous robber, he had amassed the family fortune. Sayid Shah Ibrahim, an agreeable man who lived close by, near some fish pools, was also at the fort. Ali Khan, the Sayid, and some others were busy preparing for the morrow, the tenth day of Muharram, by reading Persian religious poetry. After dinner, they excused themselves and went off to continue their reading.

The next morning, I got up later than usual and went to the fish pools with Sayid Shah Ibrahim. Three fairly small pools, and a large spring regarded as the source of the Kabul river, lay close to a hamlet below a rocky spur surmounted by a ruined fort. I had previously visited these pools in October 1952, at the end of my journey in Chitral. They were packed with enormous numbers of fish, a species of barbel, most of them weighing between half a pound and a pound. These fish were regarded as sacred and protected by ancient custom; none were permitted to be caught above the mill a little way down-stream.

Approaching one of the pools was a strange, startling experience. As we reached the water's edge a seemingly solid black wave of fish surged towards us in the hopes of food. When I tossed some food into the pool it became at once a seething mass of fish so closely packed that the smaller ones were frequently thrust up out of the water. The fish, it was said, disappeared completely for three months every spring.

The home village of Sayid Muhammad Ali Agha, our pony-man, lay about an hour's walk beyond Sar-i-Chashma. From here on the valley was heavily wooded, with high mountains on either side; a little snow lay on one 13,000-foot mountain to the south-west. The Maidan, on the southern side of the Unai Kotal, presented a striking contrast with the neighbouring Hazarajat. Apples, apricots and mulberries grew in the orchards and, on the valley floor, willows, poplars and plane trees, besides almond and walnut. Even the hillsides had a covering of bushes. While we were having lunch in an orchard near the Agha's house, a thunderstorm broke overhead, bringing a little rain.

The changing weather had produced interesting effects of light and shade, and I spent most of the afternoon taking photographs. After that I went up the hillside above the Agha's house, sat on a rock eating dried apricots and admired the fine views up and down the valley.

The following morning we left at 7.15 AM and, after about an hour, turned up the Sanglakh valley. We stopped at Changran, a pleasing spot, where the prime minister had a garden. An Uzbek family, refugees from Bokhara, were in charge, and the garden with apple trees, pear trees and flowers and an avenue of large poplars along the stream, was tended by Hazaras.

I photographed the Uzbeks and the Hazaras, and some Mongol nomads, five of whose tents were nearby. Later in the morning Jan Baz's employer, the director of the press department, a sort of head of public relations and an important man, turned up in a car with a party. I was glad to meet him: as a result of a favourable report of our journey from Jan Baz, the Afghan government gave me permission the following year to travel in Nuristan.

The Sanglakh valley was inhabited by smiling, welcoming Sayids. Everywhere along the way they asked us to stop for a cup of tea, or pressed us to spend the night. How different from the Sayids in the Hazarajat.

About two hours' march further down the valley from Changran, we halted at 5 PM in a poor village, where the road ahead divided. Having decided to follow the longer route, accompanied by a kind, helpful young Sayid, we continued walking until sunset when we reached Armun. Here we slept on a roof in the moonlight with high mountains all round us.

The villagers in Armun advised us to go back half a mile and follow the track up the last valley we had passed; this, they assured us, was the best route. Next morning we left at dawn and after a long, sometimes difficult climb over rocks and scree, got to the watershed at the top of the valley. This country looked far wilder than any I had seen in the Hazarajat; steep mountainsides riven by narrow, deep gorges and, through a haze, the towering mass of Kuh-i-Baba. God help us, I thought, if we were to be forced down into one of the Helmand's tributaries.

We made our way along the watershed, climbing gradually,

pausing occasionally while I collected various plants and small flowers; then rested, sheltered from a cold east wind by some rocks, to eat some dry bread and apples. The head of the Koli Barit valley lay directly below the summit, down a very steep incline covered with rocks and scree. There was no visible track, and consequently we had a hard job getting our pony down to the valley. As we scrambled and slithered downhill we disturbed a covey of seven snow-cock which took flight just below us and sailed out over the valley.

At the bottom, we followed a stream for half an hour until we came to some Kuchi tents. It was cold here and the Kuchis, Ibrahim Khel, provided us with bedding.

The Hazaras of the Koli Barit valley, in Surkh-o-Parsa, were now camped in their fields in black tents or, in some cases, circular dwellings like yurts made of a framework of willow saplings covered with mats and branches. One Hazara told me that they moved out of their houses to escape from the bugs, but others said they did this every autumn to allow their livestock to manure the harvested fields when they were brought inside the tents at night and kept tied up until morning. By constantly moving the site of their tents, they were able to manure the greater part of their fields: all the fields were small, the valleys on the northern slopes of the Paghman range being steep and narrow.

The Hazaras in this area were Sunni Muslims. They looked quite different, of a larger build, with less pronounced Mongol features, compared to others I had seen. Most of the men had large beards, unlike the wisps grown by most of the men in the Hazarajat.

Throughout my journey I had come across very few shrines, but here, among the neighbouring Sunnis, I saw many more shrines decorated with votive offerings of small ibex horns. None of these Hazaras appeared to be in the least fanatical and nowhere did I sense any hostility to me as a Christian.

At the junction of the Koli Barit and Colom Bela valleys, we stopped at some Hazara tents. From there we marched up the valley of Colom Bela, then up a side-valley, where we camped on the hillside near a solitary house. Coming up the Colom Bela, I noticed a tall, solid stone building like a monastery, evidently divided into separate dwellings whose windows looked out from the high wall. Further along I saw another curious sight, a sort of natural rock gateway where the Colom Bela stream had cut through granite cliffs, producing some oddly shaped pinnacles.

That evening Jan Baz and I decided to climb up and see the sacred Hauz-i-Khas pools, a place of pilgrimage near the 15,600-foot summit of Takht-i-Turkoman; meanwhile, the Sayid would take our pony from Colom Bela, directly over the pass, to Paghman. We would have to come down by way of Shakar Dara, as we had been told that, owing to sheer cliffs, there was no way of getting round the pools to the Paghman Pass.

It was bitterly cold when Jan Baz and I started off at day-break up the valley. The Hazaras in Colom Bela had asked too high a price to show us the way to the pools, but an Ibrahim Khel from a Kuchi encampment higher up came with us. At this altitude the mountain streams were frozen over.

After a long, steep scramble, which, though tiring, had not been very difficult, we arrived at the pools, a thousand feet or so below the summit of Takht-i-Turkoman. Two of them were the size of small ponds; the third, and largest, which had some mallard swimming about on it, was about 120 yards across. The pools had been formed by melted snow; in consequence their dimensions varied considerably according to the season. The pools were ringed round, except on the north-east, by granite cliffs and scree streaked with snow, and lay among a tumbled mass of granite boulders and slabs covered with a very dark, almost black patina, which from a distance looked volcanic. Nearby were several small springs, and patches of fresh green grass dotted with flowers including a sort of Canterbury bell.

Every year Hindus from Kabul made a pilgrimage to Hauz-i-Khas. Ten days before we arrived more than a hundred of them, and for the first time some Sikhs, had undertaken this pilgrimage. They had spent two nights beside the pools, 14,000 feet above sea-level; getting there must have been a stiff climb for a Hindu shopkeeper.

Jan Baz and I climbed with some effort up a rough, boulder-strewn face to the summit of Takht-i-Turkoman. Despite the hazy atmosphere, which diminished a magnificent view, I could still discern the outline of the distant Nuristan mountains.

A fairly steep descent brought us down to the Dara valley by early afternoon. In my diary I wrote: '[we found] a lot of snow lying in the head of the valley in the stream bed. The valley bottom was bloody going, a jumble of boulders, with occasional goat tracks which petered out almost at once'.

On our way down the valley we passed encampments of Kuchis, who gave us tea and bread. They owned the wheatfields, surrounded by low, stone walls, in which they pitched their tents. At five o'clock we stopped in the first village we came to, where we stayed with a Pathan who had married a cousin of Jan Baz. The Pathan and his five brothers lived together in a house built round a square courtyard with the windows opening on to it. Jan Baz's cousin came in and sat with us for a bit; afterwards we went out into the garden and ate plums, apples and grapes. The family gave us a good dinner, including some excellent curds, in a small room on the upper floor. The shiny white plasterwork decorated with coloured, incised patterns was typical of any Pathan dwelling. The room, with a baby's cot slung across the middle, felt rather crowded.

On 15 September we arrived in Kabul where I stayed once again with Sir David Lascelles at the British Embassy. Two days later I travelled in the embassy bus to Peshawar, and from there on 19 September I took the overnight train to Karachi.

One afternoon, in November 1996, the telephone rang in my Chelsea flat. When I answered it, a voice said: 'This is Jan Baz. Do you remember me? I travelled with you in the Hazarajat.' After forty-two years I was naturally surprised, but delighted. I asked: 'Where are you now? And how did you know where to find me?' He said: 'I am here in London, visiting some friends from Afghanistan. Yours was the only English name I knew. After I arrived I went to the British Museum and enquired about you. They sent me to the Natural History Museum, and they gave me your address and your telephone number.' I said: 'This is splendid. Come round as soon as you can.'

We spent the rest of the day together, talking about our journey in the Hazarajat, which Jan Baz remembered vividly, and everything that had happened to us since then. That evening I gave him dinner at a nearby restaurant, and the following week, shortly before he returned to Kabul, Jan Baz invited me to dine with him and his Afghan hosts in Shepherd's Bush.

The success of my journey in the Hazarajat had been due very largely to the patience and tact of Jan Baz, under conditions which were always primitive and often exasperating. He was invariably cheerful, obliging and interesting, and his company was a constant pleasure.

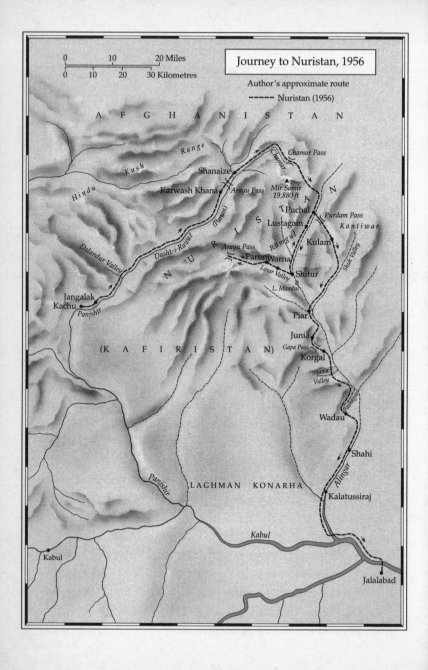

Journey to Nuristan, 1956

Author's approximate route
----- Nuristan (1956)

0   10   20 Miles
0 10 20 30 Kilometres

A F G H A N I S T A N

Hindu   Kush   Range   Chamar   Chamar Pass

Shanaize
Karwash Khana   Arayu Pass
Mir Samir
19,880 ft
Puchal   Purdam Pass
Lustagam   Kantiwar
Kulam
Dolandur Valley   Dasht-i-Ravat   Arayu Pass   Parun Warna   Shuk Valley
Linar Valley   Shitur
L. Mandul

Jangalak
Kachu   Panjshir

Piar

Junia
Gapa Pass
Korgal

(K A F I R I S T A N)   Shania
Valley

Dashtgem

Wadau

Shahi

Panjshir   LAGHMAN   KONARHA   Alingar   Kalatussiraj

Kabul   Kabul

Jalalabad

NURISTAN I

1956

I HAD BEEN ANXIOUS to travel in Nuristan ever since I visited the Kafirs in Chitral in 1952. Permission to go there had always been difficult to obtain from the Afghan government; but after my subsequent journey in the Hazarajat I received this long-awaited permission in the summer of 1955. By then I had decided to travel in the High Atlas in Morocco. I arranged, however, to go to Nuristan in July the following year.

Nuristan is the little-known area of the Hindu Kush which lies inside Afghanistan to the north of Jalalabad along the Chitral border. Comparatively few Europeans have travelled in Nuristan: in 1826 and 1828 Colonel Alexander Gardner, a soldier of fortune, twice passed through Kafiristan, 'Land of Unbelievers', as it was then known; in 1883 W. W. MacNair visited the Bashgul valley. This valley was more thoroughly explored in 1885 by Colonel Woodthorpe of the Indian Survey, accompanied by Sir William Lockhart. These appear to have been the only Europeans to travel in this country until Sir George Scott Robertson spent a year in the Bashgul valley in 1889–90, while serving as a British agent in Chitral. Nuristan, or Kafiristan, was then independent: in 1888 Kipling wrote his powerful story 'The Man who would be King' about this country.

In 1893, however, Sir Mortimer Durand reached an agreement with Abd er Rahman, the Amir of Afghanistan, about the frontier between India and Afghanistan, and by this agreement the former Kafiristan fell almost entirely within Afghanistan. Only a small area remained inside Chitral, the area inhabited to this day by the Black Kafirs. The other Kafirs (as the inhabitants of Kafiristan were known) were forcibly converted to Islam when Abd er Rahman overran their country in the winter of 1895–96, in a skilfully conducted campaign which lasted only four months. Two important German expeditions travelled extensively in Nuristan in 1928 and 1935, and more recently an expedition from Denmark – when I went there in 1956 the Nuristanis referred to all Europeans as Germans.

There has been some debate as to the origin of the Nuristanis, who evidently belong to the Dardic branch of the Indo-European family. Some authorities have suggested that they are descendants of Greek garrisons left behind by Alexander, when that god-like figure swept like a comet across the world and passed down the Alingar valley. Others maintain that the ancestors of the Nuristanis were there three thousand years ago, long before Alexander.

After visiting the Black Kafir valleys in Chitral, I had acquired Robertson's book, *The Kafirs of the Hindu Kush* (1896). He admired their reckless bravery, their powers of physical endurance and their hospitality, but he deplored the pride they took in killing, whether man, woman or child. He also wrote that it was 'as natural for them to steal as to eat', and that 'their avarice was almost a mental disease'. I noticed that his map showed in some detail the configuration of all Kafiristan, large areas of which none of these early travellers had visited. Gardner, escaping to Yarkand after his party had been massacred, would scarcely have mapped the area through which he passed. I realized that the work must have been done by those dauntless, anonymous individuals, Indian as well as British, who worked for the Survey of India and, at risk to their lives, mapped the country across the border.

The Natural History Museum's Botanical Department had asked me to collect plant specimens in Nuristan. John Newbould, a qualified botanist who had been with me in Morocco, hoped to accompany me to Nuristan. We agreed that John would collect these plants for the Museum and would bring the necessary materials, besides an aneroid and other instruments with him to Afghanistan. But when I emerged from the Marshes of southern Iraq, where I had spent the spring and early summer of 1956, I learnt that the Afghan government had refused to give him an entry visa. I knew that there were presses and blotting paper in Kabul, left over from my journey in the Hazarajat; there was, however, no time to get the other equipment sent out from England.

I arrived in Kabul on 19 July, and stayed with Ken Dulling at the British Embassy. My arrival coincided with the Eid festival, marking the end of Ramadan, when all the government offices were shut, and in consequence it took me ten days to get the necessary travel permit to visit Nuristan. The Faculty of Literature kindly allowed one of their students, a young Pathan named Abd al Nawab, to go with me as my interpreter.

On 28 July I left Kabul after lunch and drove with Clifford Jupp of the British Embassy and Abd al Nawab up the Panjshir valley as far as Kachu, a distance of 70 miles.

At Jangalak, two miles from Kachu at the end of the motor-road, I engaged a Tajik boy, called Zeman, to cook and two other Tajiks with two ponies to carry our baggage. I had been assured that it was possible for horses to cross the Hindu Kush into Nuristan and to travel down the Ramgul valley at least as far as Puchal. This proved to be so, but I should have done far better to have taken Tajik porters from the Panjshir, and to have kept them with me all the time I was in Nuristan, instead of relying upon Nuristani porters when we eventually sent the ponies back.

We travelled for the next five days up the Panjshir valley. The bare, steep, scree-covered mountains flanking this narrow valley swept down almost to the edge of the river, which was deep and swift-flowing. Bridges across the Panjshir river were few and far between. There were small villages and scattered farmsteads with patches of Indian corn; the wheat and barley crops had already been harvested. Clumps of poplar grew along the river, and there were mulberry trees everywhere, covered with ripe, sweet, white berries.

The Panjshir valley was inhabited by Tajiks, who wore long, coloured cloaks of striped material, and often waistcoats, over white shirts and trousers. Most of the men wore turbans, white, black or pale-blue in colour, but a few wore only skull caps. Some of the older men I saw at Barak had thin, wispy beards; others had distinctive, flat Mongol features. All the Tajiks in Panjshir were Sunnis, as were a colony of Hazaras living in Dara Hazara, a side-valley coming from the east, between the villages of Barak and Marz.

The main caravan route to Badakshan followed the Panjshir valley; this my men always referred to as the road to Turkistan.

At Marz, a large village opposite a ruined fort, I saw houses and shrines decorated with the horns of ibex; these, I was told, were fairly common. We halted briefly in Marz, then marched on to Char Karia where we camped for the night in a small, ter-raced orchard, under a canopy of mulberry trees. The Tajiks at Char Karia were friendly, but inhospitable by any standards. They gave us nothing to eat except mulberries, which they shook down into a wide cloth held between two poles.

The next day we set off at 7 AM, in a strong following wind which kept blowing throughout the day. In the larger villages, such as Khanj, Matah and Safaidchi, we usually stopped at a *shai kana*, or tea-shop, sometimes for a cup of tea but more often so that my companions could inhale a few quick puffs from a hubble-bubble.

The further we went up the valley, the less inhabited it became: after Safaidchi, we passed smaller villages where the people were harvesting tiny patches of wheat. The foothills on either side hid the high, precipitous mountains which lay behind them and only occasionally, as we passed a side-valley, did we catch a glimpse of the snow.

By the middle of the afternoon we reached the beginning of a cultivated stretch, known as Dasht-i-Rawat, just beyond the mouth of the Dalandur valley. We rested here on green grass, beside a shai kana, near a small waterfall; a very pleasant spot where the people were friendly. Some way further on I discovered that, when my Tajiks were reloading one of the ponies, they had left behind my goat-skin bag containing spare lenses and films. They immediately went back and, luckily, found the bag which a man had put in his house for safety.

A variety of crops and fruit flourished in Dasht-i-Rawat where a ribbon of small terraced fields and orchards followed the river for several miles, as far as Karwash Khana. Here, the locals cultivated wheat, barley, maize, vetch, clover and beans; and as well as the ubiquitous mulberries they grew apples, apricots and walnuts.

The following morning, after marching for an hour-and-a-half, we crossed a low pass at the end of Dasht-i-Rawat, and carried on through barren, stony hills which were rocky in places and steep. A big side-valley, with villages and cultivation in it, joined the Panjshir from the east; a pass at the head of this valley, which led over into Nuristan, was said to be steep and difficult.

On the way to Karwash Khana, we were joined by some nomad Pathans, two Tajiks with harp-like instruments which they used to card cotton, and a small Tajik boy on a horse. We arrived at Karwash Khana by mid-morning, where the only dwelling was a square, stone-built house, roofed with shrubs laid on poles and covered with some earth; it was primitive and very dark inside. Below the house lay a few tiny fields of Indian corn and a little wheat. The friendly owner, who had a little son aged about seven, gave us freshly made bread for lunch.

A short stretch of the river beyond Karwash Khana, known as the Parian, rushed down between high, barren, treeless mountains which in places were rocky and sheer. The first of two parallel valleys, both known as Arayu, joined the main valley after a few miles; streams of muddy glacier water flowed down this first valley, but the main stream itself was clear. The second valley came in opposite Shanaize, where there was a village and some cultivation. Here I met the writer Eric Newby, and his companion, Hugh Carless: exhausted, desiccated, wind-chapped, lame, with bandaged hands, they looked in thoroughly bad shape. They had spent the previous three weeks trying to climb, with inadequate equipment, the 20,000-foot Mir Samir that loomed at the head of the valley. They were too small a party and the locals had refused to carry loads on the mountain; as a result Newby and Carless had been unable to camp high enough up. After a valiant but unsuccessful attempt to reach the summit, they had travelled down to Punchal, in Nuristan, and come back to Panjshir over the Arayu Pass. We spent a pleasant evening in Shanaize, camped together in an orchard, and I got some very useful information from them about the country ahead of me. Newby later included an amusing description of our meeting in *A Short Walk in the Hindu Kush*.

We started at 7.30 AM the next morning, soon after Newby and Carless had left, and walked on through a continuous narrow strip of wheat, barley and bean-fields as far as Gishta. Until now we had been travelling along the west bank of the Panjshir, but just beyond Gishta we crossed the river by a narrow, wobbly bridge which the ponies walked over without hesitation. An hour later we arrived at Char-i-Balan, a cluster of adjoining houses, on a hill above the valley; from a distance the village looked, to me, like a fort.

We spent the night in the guest-room of a house owned by hospitable Tajiks who gave us tea and a dinner of bread with milk and butter. These Tajiks seemed to be a distinctive type, bearded, but not Mongol-looking. Some of them wore high boots made of soft leather. Like the Hazaras, each family carried down from the steep mountainsides bundles of winter fodder which they stored on the village's communal roof. Occasional patches of green showed on these otherwise bare, tawny slopes wherever there was a spring.

The following morning we came to Pase Akib village, where the Panjshir ended at the junction of two valleys: the Margadal, which came down from the Anjuman Pass; and the Chamar with a pass at the head of it into Nuristan. After we had passed Ishander Beg, a village less than half-an-hour's walk from Pase Akib, we turned eastwards up the Chamar valley.

On the steep slopes at this end of the Chamar valley there were small fields of wheat, and channels along the mountainside carrying water to the cultivations further down the

Panjshir. We followed the valley bottom which was covered with green turf, except where it was buried under scree and other debris from old landslides. The mountains on either side were precipitous and rocky with some snow along their tops. We were now too high for permanent villages. Here the valley was only inhabited during the summer, when both Tajiks and Kuchis took their herds up there for the grazing.

Towards midday we came to some Kuchi encampments belonging to the Chanzai tribe. Later on we passed more Kuchi tents, and camels high up on the steep mountainsides above them. I saw two lammergeyers soaring above the valley, and a few choughs. An hour before nightfall we stopped at an ailoq belonging to a friendly Tajik, Mir Sadat Khan, where there were horses, donkeys, sheep, goats – one of which we bought – and some dogs. The ailoq consisted of stone shelters, roofed with poles and shrubs, built among rocks near a spring. The rocks had been part of an old landslide. Mir Sadat Khan had no cups or kettles at his ailoq, nor indeed anything but the absolute necessities. Likewise few Nuristanis owned a kettle. Apart from the iron cooking pots, many of their household utensils, such as milk pails, were made of wood, often deco-rated with crude incised patterns.

Up here, it was cold by sunset and we slept in our small Meade tent.

The following morning we continued up the valley, with the snow-covered summit of Mir Samir almost immediately above us. I took several photographs of the mountain, its sheer rock-faces and a small glacier, some with my 135mm telephoto lens.

Every day the atmosphere had been hazy, but now for the first time the weather cleared and the Chamar looked green and very pleasant. As we went along, I collected more flowers; primulas were already over, but I found many others by the river near a series of small cascades. Not far from here we stopped at another ailoq with only women and girls in it. None of them would come near us and I suspected Newby had been trying to photograph them. When we had met at Shanaize, Newby told me that he had had a lot of difficulty photographing the girls; this was inevitable since all these people were Muslims. To the south-west a precipitous, jagged ridge with some small glaciers connected the Mir Samir ridge on one side and the pass on the other. Here the Chamar river rose in a small lake. In the evening a little cloud gathered; some snow fell at sunset, but, owing to the sloping ground, we could find nowhere suitable for the tent.

On 4 August after a cloudy start, the weather gradually cleared and the morning turned out fine, warm and sunny. We forded the stream and then continued on up the mountain to the Chamar Pass. The going, in places, was steep but nowhere difficult, even for our ponies. We passed a small tarn, about 50 yards across, and reached the top of the 16,500-foot-high pass shortly before 11 o'clock. From the pass we had a magnificent view of Mir Samir, its snow-covered summit brilliantly white against the clear blue sky, but I was surprised to see how little snow there was on the surrounding mountains; near the pass I saw only a few drifts.

We dropped steeply down into the Ramgul valley on the far side, also known locally as the Chamar, and camped in an empty ailoq. On the way down I collected more plants. I could see no trees or bushes anywhere; the only fuel here was pincushion vegetation and cow dung, plentiful round the ailoq.

Abd al Nawab and our Tajik ponymen had admitted they

feared the Nuristanis, who, they said, resented Newby's and Carless's visit; they anticipated that we might have trouble when we met them. Towards evening half a dozen Nuristanis turned up in our camp; they had seen us in the distance and had come down from their ailoq further up the valley to find out who we were. The Nuristanis were very friendly; they invited us to come and spend the night with them, and, when we declined their invitation, they settled down to entertain us by dancing and singing. Their music reminded me of songs and dances that I had heard and seen previously in Chitral. In appearance they were like handsome Europeans, light in colour, with brown hair and beards; several of them had grey eyes. All of them wore dark Chitrali caps, short, dark-coloured overcoats which ended in a distinctive, tasselled fringe at the hem, thick, dark, homespun trousers and puttees. They had red scarves knotted round their throats, and all of them were barefoot.

They remained with us until sunset and then, after inviting us to visit them next day, they left, moving away quickly and easily across some very broken ground. I realized that these people were born mountaineers and would make magnificent porters. Later, I would see men carrying loads of butter from their ailoqs down to the villages, travelling at a jog-trot although each of them must have been carrying a load weighing 50 pounds or more. The men carried the butter in skins fastened on their backs inside a V-shaped frame made from two sticks. Sometimes men, women and children carried loads of firewood on their backs in large, V-shaped baskets.

After a warm, still night, the following day dawned bright and clear. The evenings before that had been bitterly cold by sunset, but here I sat about without a blanket until I went to bed.

Leaving Abd al Nawab, the Tajiks, ponies and kit behind at the ailoq, I set off early to climb by myself to the top of the ridge, above the source of the Ramgul river. This involved a fairly steep scramble. There was no snow, although the ridge was about the same altitude as the Chamar Pass. I took a long time getting back and, on the way, I met Abd al Nawab and the two Tajiks who had come in search of me. It was far warmer, and a lot greener, on this side of the mountain; indeed, the difference in temperature on its north and south sides was very marked. Nowhere in Nuristan did I see any significant glaciers, although there were the moraines of old glaciers in all the high valleys.

On our way back to camp, the Nuristanis we had met the day before urged us to stop at their ailoq for curds and milk. I had already used up more than four spools of film coming up the Panjshir and Chamar valleys, and at this ailoq I finished a fifth spool. These Nuristanis loved being photographed.

Some nomads, called Gujurs, had camped nearby. These Gujurs, who wore turbans, looked very Indian beside the Nuristanis; thieving, lawless and continually on the move, they had a bad reputation and were universally unpopular in this country. I was told that they spent the summers in the mountains, as far north as Dani Munjan, and wintered in the southern valleys near Laghman. The Nuristanis from the ailoq went down and took two goats off them as tribute.

At first the river idled through green, grassy meadows; then, as the valley sloped sharply downhill, the slow-flowing stream became a rushing torrent. The mountains, covered with scree and eroded rock, rose up steeply on both sides. There were no precipices here, but falls of rock extending right across the valley made the going difficult for our ponies. Near the confluence of two mountain streams, one of which flowed down from Mir Samir, I noticed some juniper, the first I had seen, and a lot of dwarf rose bushes. All the time, as we went along, I heard the high-pitched alarm calls of marmots among the rocks; their cries reminded me of a boy blowing a pea-whistle.

We camped for the night at about 12,000 feet, beside an ailoq occupied by three young Nuristanis. These men treated us churlishly and refused to let us have either milk or butter. I discovered that in Nuristan it was always difficult to buy flour and this made travelling with porters difficult. It was even more difficult, however, to buy butter, although the Nuristanis produced large quantities in their summer camps. Whenever we enquired, they invariably said that the butter did not belong only to them but was the joint produce of several families. Butter was kept submerged in an icy-cold stream for twenty or twenty-five days, and then taken down from the ailoqs to the villages and boiled. Later it would be carried down to Laghman, or across the Hindu Kush to Panjshir, for sale.

Although the Nuristanis did not seem to own large flocks of sheep or goats, nor have many cows, during the summer months spent on the high pastures, a single family might produce between 40 and 50 seers of butter, approximately the equivalent of 80–100 pounds.

At midday we had finished what was left of the goat I had bought from Mir Sadat Khan on 2 August, and that night we had nothing to eat but dry bread. Some heavy clouds gathered during the afternoon, and the evening stayed warm with occasional flashes of lightning at the horizon to the east.

By 7 AM the following morning we were marching along the river, by now quite a fair-sized stream, rushing down through a long, precipitous rocky gorge. As we descended the valley we came to more scattered juniper, then thickets of birch, wild currant and, still lower down, willows and tamarisks along the river banks. We crossed a plank bridge, and then two more bridges in rapid succession. The bridges were fashioned from juniper trunks, split in half and more than twenty feet in length. As I watched our ponies crossing and re-crossing the river, I felt increasingly anxious that the loads, especially my collection of plants, might get wet.

We passed a Nuristani family, going up the valley, who gave us some fresh apricots. There were three women in the party, and a thirteen-year-old boy who cried when I took a photograph of him.

Further down the valley we had to cross two more bridges. We then climbed from the gorge up a mountainside on our right. Here the Chamar entered the Bugulchi, or Dara Rast, above Puchal, and there the river was generally known as the Puchal. Names were confusing in Nuristan since they had abandoned some of the old Kafir names. The whole of this valley was the Ramgul, and the tribes who lived here were also called the Ramgul, but today many of the younger men did not know this name and called themselves Nuristanis. The valley to the east was the Kulam, and both the valley and the tribes who lived there were still called by this name. Still further to the east they also used the old names, Kti or Kantiwar, Presun and Waigal.

At the time I wrote: 'This is terrific country.' The scenery round Puchal, indeed, was magnificent – the valley very narrow with the mountains rising above it, jagged and sheer; their lower slopes, with farmsteads and wheat fields, thickly wooded with holly-oak. We marched steadily along the mountainside, about 1,000 feet above the valley, before descending to Puchal, but we were delayed when Abd al Nawab, who had wandered off by himself, got lost and took half an hour to catch up with us. In spite of this delay, we arrived before nightfall.

Puchal, the chief village in the Ramgul valley, was divided into two settlements and numbered in all about forty houses. We stopped at the first group of a dozen flat-roofed, two-storeyed, stone and mud dwellings, where a friendly Nuristani put us up in a small, clean guest-room with carpets on the floor. Here I noticed a chair had the back-rest made from two large ibex horns. Like most other Nuristani houses, this one was sparsely furnished and remarkably free of bugs, a pleasant contrast to the Kafir villages in Chitral where the bugs had been appalling.

Puchal, with its three mosques, was the religious centre for the district. The moment the call to sunset prayers sounded, everyone including the children flocked to pray; but whereas the mullahs and elders were fanatical, the ordinary people were not, although they said their prayers with great regularity. Nowhere have I heard so many calls to prayer as I did in these Nuristani villages, the words almost unintelligible, a strange travesty of the original Arabic.

The mullahs in Puchal made no secret of their hostility to me as a Christian. When I returned here for the third time, a fortnight later, after an unsuccessful attempt to get into the Kulam valley from the Wanasgul, a mullah rushed down the hillside towards us and poured out curses on me for defiling this stronghold of Islam with my presence. This was the fanaticism of the newly converted; his father must have been an infidel, for the country had only been converted to Islam sixty years before.

That evening our host gave us a dinner of bread and eggs. The almost invariable diet of these Nuristanis was bread, made from wheat, barley or maize, eaten with curds or cheese. They kept some chickens and ate eggs; they also ate fish, despite Robertson's assertion that the tribes in the Bashgul would not eat fish under any circumstances. Like the Hazaras, when they killed off any surplus livestock at the beginning of the winter, they would eat a certain amount of meat, but while I was in Nuristan in their houses I was never given any meat, other than chicken.

Next morning we passed through the larger of the two settlements constituting Puchal, about thirty houses clinging to the hillside above the river. The better-off houses were warmed in winter by means of hot air from a fire, conducted to the rooms by flues built under the floors. Some houses had large floor-to-ceiling windows on both sides of the rooms, with vertical sliding shutters or shutters that opened inwards.

Accompanied by our host, Abd al Nawab and I left the Tajiks to cross the river with the ponies, and made our way slowly past some outlying houses scattered among orchards and fields of wheat and maize. Everyone we met shook hands with us, and all seemed friendly and welcoming. We stopped for an hour to allow the Tajiks and ponies to catch up, then we carried on down the valley past a cemetery with several shrines in it, and other graves, probably sites connected with their former pagan worship. Here, I was especially aware of their recent conversion. This may have been due to the similarity between this country and the Black Kafir valleys in Chitral.

At Lustagam, we met Dost Muhammad Khan, the son of a general based in Kabul, who took us to his uncle's house for lunch. We spent the rest of the day there, and that night we slept in Dost Muhammad Khan's nearby house. An elderly but still active villager turned up who claimed to be one hundred and twenty years old. He told us that he had been twenty-five when he fought against Abd er Rahman, which meant that he was, in fact, now aged about ninety.

One of the men in Dost Muhammad Khan's house had shot three bears, while another man claimed to have shot ten. Both black and brown bears were to be found in Nuristan. Black bears were common and did considerable damage to the villagers' crops, especially the maize. They would also steal the butter left to cool in streams near the ailoqs. At Lustagam, bears raided the fields close to the village at night.

The next morning soon after we left Lustagam, the Nuristani who had joined us near the Chamar Pass started to argue with one of our Tajik ponymen who, he insisted, owed him a twelve-year-old debt for his share of the sale of a cow. The argument had gone on for some time when suddenly, on a narrow stretch of the path, the Nuristani struck the Tajik to the ground, where he lay weeping with blood streaming from his nose. When I arrived on the scene, the Nuristani had just kicked the Tajik, and was about to do so again. I threw him back and threatened to hit him unless he calmed down; then, using Nawab as my interpreter, I told him that the question of the debt must be settled by discussion and not by violence. The Nuristani swore on the Koran that he was owed the money, which was undoubtedly true, and Abd al Nawab, who handled the situation with skill, made the Tajik pay it over. The two men eventually parted in quite a friendly manner.

The Nuristanis were temperamental and erratic: they frequently raced about or flung themselves on the ground; they would ask innumerable questions, then suddenly lose interest. I sensed a streak of unpredictable violence in their nature, which the Nuristani's attack on our Tajik ponyman confirmed.

About six miles down the valley from Puchal, we passed

Sang-i-Navishta, where a rock beside the track bore an inscription by Abd er Rahman celebrating his conquest of Kafiristan, and another inscription attributed by the locals to Timurleng who passed through this country in 1398. The names and inscriptions were etched faintly, high up on the rock; this, and the sun shining directly on the rock face, made them difficult to see and impossible to photograph.

We arrived shortly before midday in Mangur. From there, we had some difficulty following the track which meandered through small terraced fields with fruit trees growing round them, so that we seemed to be walking through one more-or-less continuous orchard.

The narrow valley, flanked by wooded slopes rising steeply from the river, left little room for the fields, scattered farmsteads and small villages. Most of the villages had a mosque, consisting of a single rectangular room, and everywhere the muezzin sounded for each of the five daily prayers. We camped beside a house midway between Mangur and Gadwal and, in the evening, we were joined by a crowd of boys who sang and danced to tunes, played on a reed pipe, which sounded sweet and very clear, like birdsong.

By the time we started the next morning women were already out reaping wheat in a field below the house. We went on down the valley, past Gadwal, to Shitur where the Linar valley entered the Ramgul from the north. A steep climb for two hours over the mountainside brought us to Parun, a fair-sized village some five hundred feet above the Linar, where we slept on the roof of a mosque. This part of the country seemed unusually dry, and there was no water in any of the gullies. At Parun they told us that hardly any snow had fallen the previous winter, and very little the winter before that.

One of the villagers gave us corn-cakes and mutton for dinner. The meat tasted very good, but I suspected that it had come from a dying sheep as the animal had been slaughtered before we arrived. Besides maize, apricots and apples, the villagers grew a variety of mulberry with large black berries the size of a loganberry. Some of this fruit was harvested and dried on the house roofs, along with hay and the stacks of rhubarb leaves gathered on the mountain and used for winter fodder. But most of the mulberries were left to rot on the ground where they fell. The Nuristanis were lazy about collecting fruit, most of which was of poor quality, and I was often struck by the strong smell of fermenting mulberries and other fruit when I walked through their orchards.

High, rocky mountains rose straight up out of the Linar valley all round us, their awesome jagged peaks, lit at intervals by the sun, silhouetted against masses of broken grey cloud.

We left Parun at 8 A M and followed the mountain track to the junction with Muchim Kunda, or Deshtir, a large side-valley which branched north-east from the Linar. There was a plank bridge here but, despite constant warnings, Kake, one of the Tajiks, instead of unloading his pony, plunged it into the stream which was so deep that the water came up to my boxes. In consequence of the row which ensued, I decided to dismiss the Tajiks and get pack ponies from the Nuristanis.

Further up the Linar, we rested the ponies and lunched at Shalai Dir; then we went on as far as Bisiaider, a larger village, with terraced fields just below the tree-line, where we camped on the flat roof of a house.

Most of the Nuristanis in this village dressed like Tajiks and, instead of Nuristani caps, wore turbans. Even in 1889 Robertson noted that the Kafirs had no particular dress of their own, but wore indiscriminately the clothes of neighbouring tribes, and this was especially true today. Some of them dressed like Tajiks, others like Pathans. They wore Chitrali caps, turbans or skull caps as the fancy took them. Their only indigenous dress seemed to be the men's fringed overcoat, and the habit of wearing gay-coloured scarves knotted round their throats. Many of them sewed charms and coins on to their jackets. The young men and boys painted their eyes with a red juice and also used antimony on their eyelids, which gave them a strange and rather dissipated appearance. The Nuristani women did not veil, but were extremely shy, turning away or hiding themselves whenever I drew near. They were fond of red as a colour, especially for their under-garments. The boys often carried double-stringed bows, like those I had seen in Chitral, for shooting stones, and spent much of their time shooting at birds, although they seldom hit any.

In the evening the villagers sang and danced, accompanied by a two-stringed viol or else by rhythmic hand-clapping. Two boys performed a type of dance I had previously seen near Mangur, whose movements were mainly confined to the body and arms. Then a man got up and danced to frenzied singing and clapping, spinning round, throwing out his arms, separating and closing his legs and sometimes squatting down.

In the morning I paid off the Tajiks and engaged two Nuristanis with two ponies. The Nuristanis had to fetch their ponies, both of which were unshod, down from the high pastures, and this delayed us until well into the afternoon. We arrived at Atcha Giour, the last village to the west up the Linar valley, and here we stopped for the night.

After dinner, a lad with heavily painted eyes danced and then sang to the viol which I thought he played remarkably well; the villagers sometimes played a viol with three or five strings, similar to the instruments I had seen in Chitral. The songs were mostly Persian, but the villagers also sang their own Nuristani songs. All of them were tuneful, often rather melancholy, with curious rippling melodies. The Nuristanis were nearly all bilingual, speaking Persian as well as their own language which has several dialects. The people of Ramgul, Kulam and Kantiwar spoke the same dialect, which differed from those spoken in Pech and in the Bashgul valley. In fact, during this journey we met few people who could not speak Persian, although practically none of them spoke Pushtu, the language of Afghanistan.

That night we slept on a roof, a very pleasant spot, with a good view down the mountainsides lit by the moon which was now in its first quarter.

I woke to find the valley wreathed in mist and clouds low down over the mountains. We left soon after sunrise and followed the stream, fringed by juniper, willow, birch and white-leafed poplar, until the valley divided; then we continued up the right branch to some ailoqs immediately below the Arayu Pass. A small girl of about seven, with pale blue eyes, came with us as far as the ailoqs. The sweet little thing made nothing of her long uphill walk, even though she was carrying a basket of apples on her back.

Patches of snow lay on the mountains at the end of a valley to our left, where a pass led down to Dara Hazara, the Hazara enclave opposite Barak in the Panjshir valley.

Abd al Nawab, Zeman, our cook, and the two ponymen remained at the ailoqs, while I set off, accompanied by a Nuristani herd-boy, to climb the Arayu Pass. The track was good, but the grinding 3,000-foot haul proved too much for the young Nuristani, who soon turned back. After about three hours, I reached a small plateau at the top of the pass; a stream, flowing due north from its source on the plateau, marked the route which Newby and Carless had followed down to Shanaize. Very little snow lay on the mountains at the head of the pass, and most of the bare rock faces were nearly black in colour, or rimed with a rust-red patina. I estimated that if the valley behind me lay 12,000 feet above sea-level, the top of the Arayu Pass must be about 15,000. From the pass I got another view of Mir Samir, flecked with snow, towering high above other snow-capped mountains in the distance. I could never have gone off by myself like this on the other side of the border where in 1952 I had had to travel accompanied by an armed escort.

I descended rapidly and arrived back at the ailoqs at 3.30 PM, where I discovered that Abd al Nawab had sent Zeman after me when the Nuristani boy returned. Zeman came back an hour or so later, I could not think how I had missed him unless, perhaps, he had fallen asleep under a rock.

After a wild, windy night the weather cleared and the sky remained cloudless all day. We started early and reached Bisiaider well before noon. We had to spend the rest of the day here while the Nuristanis tried to find a blacksmith to shoe their ponies. In the evening I went up the Kamal valley opposite the village to look for plants; I found some acacia and a variety of red-berried thorn – and a mouse, one of the few mice I ever saw in Nuristan.

In the morning the Nuristanis took their ponies over the pass into Ramgul, with instructions to wait for us somewhere down by the Shitur bridge. Meanwhile, I went with Abd al Nawab and a boy from Linar to look at the Mandul lake.

We travelled fast, considering the rough going, passing the villages of Parun and Warna on the mountainside above us; on the path close to Linar, I noticed the fresh tracks of a bear. We had some difficulty crossing the Linar, just above its junction with the Ramgul, where the river rushed down over a bed of slippery boulders. Further down, at Mandul, the villagers were out harvesting their fields of hay. The Ramgul here was deep, slow-flowing and fringed by willows; the villagers had constructed a succession of breakwaters along this stretch of the river to stop it eating away at the fertile ground on the west bank.

The Ramgul flowed through the Mandul lake, which was perhaps half a mile across at its widest point; beyond it the river flowed down through a rocky gorge. The lake was said to be full of fish which the Nuristanis caught with nets. They told me they sometimes caught fish which, judging by their description, must have weighed up to 100 lbs or even more. These fish were long and narrow, dark in colour, with a mouth like a shark's but without teeth or feelers. I saw about half-a-dozen cormorants on this lake, and other birds including a griffon vulture and many magpies in its vicinity; I also found otter tracks imprinted in the coarse white sand at the water's edge. Several boys were bathing in the lake, and like all Nuristanis they were extremely good swimmers.

At Shitur, there was no sign of our ponies; we waited for them, until someone told us that they had already passed through the village. Half an hour later, we caught up with them where they had stopped by a house.

We continued up the valley, past Gadwal, as far as Genokhail where we arrived after some delay, caused by a load which had slipped, just as it was getting dark. On the way here we bought some unmilled wheat, but our flour was finished and we had great difficulty in getting any bread at Genokhail; in the end a villager produced a few broken scraps of bread which we ate for dinner.

We started off next morning at six. Aiyub, a Nuristani lad from Linar village, came with us, since one of our ponymen had disappeared.

I had now decided to continue on up the valley to Wanasgul, and to cross from there into Kantiwar and then back into the Kulam valley. Instead of spending the night in Puchal, we crossed to the opposite bank and followed a narrow track a few feet above the river. As one of the Nuristanis was leading his pony round a bend, its load snagged on a projecting rock; the pony struggled to pass, but was forced over backwards into the river. It found its feet and started out into the river, here a rushing torrent with rapids only a short distance downstream. The pony's load, meanwhile, had slipped under its belly. It would undoubtedly have drowned in the rapids if Aiyub had not immediately jumped into the river and turned it back to the bank.

On this pony were all my plant specimens, and the two boxes containing among other things spare lenses for my camera, my money, passport, spare clothes and notebooks – in fact, everything except for my bedding. My large collection of plants was reduced to a sodden mass of blotting paper. There was nowhere to camp except on the narrow, stony path and here we struggled to dry enough paper to save the sopping-wet plant collection while it was still daylight. Luckily there was only a gentle breeze instead of the strong wind which normally blew at this hour, but our task was not made easier by strings of women who came down the path carrying loads of wood. We got the last plants spread out between sheets of dry blotting-paper just as it got dark.

Next morning we marched for an hour, before turning east up the Wanasgul valley. We passed through woods of oak, willow and various kinds of thorn trees, and then through thickets of birch, scattered junipers and, to my surprise, a few tamarisks. The valley bottom was damp and very green, with a lot of plants, most of which I had already collected. Six Gujurs, four of them quite young men, carrying very heavy loads of flour, accompanied us for part of the way. They spoke a little Pushtu, but no Persian. The Gujurs had come down to Puchal some days earlier to buy wheat and have it ground at the mill; they were now on their way to Kantiwar.

Rock-falls, in places, made the going slow and difficult. We halted half-way through the morning, until mid-afternoon, to get my plants and all my other possessions thoroughly dried. That night we camped at an ailoq, high up in the valley, where the scenery was wild and magnificent, the mountains towering above us, streaked with snow. We bought a sheep from the herdsmen, and Zeman gave us a good supper with very good soup; we slept in an empty enclosure, sheltered from the cold night wind, the valley below us bathed in moonlight.

The following morning, because of the intense cold, we started late. While the men were loading their ponies, I took some photographs of the Nuristani shepherds; then, soon after 8 A M, we set off for the pass. It was a steep climb; there was no visible track, and the going was appalling for the ponies. We went up very slowly, with frequent halts to rest them. Tumbled boulders were piled on a great bed of plutonic rock, smoothed and scratched by ice, and split and riven into segments, which were often very regular. The rock, pale grey in colour, was covered with a dark, almost black patina so that it resembled basalt, typical of the rock in those parts of Nuristan which I visited. I noticed tiny ponds of water here and there among the boulders. I climbed to the top of the pass into Kantiwar, but it was quite impossible to get the ponies through this chaos of tumbled rocks.

Eventually, as it was getting dark, we managed to get the ponies across another pass on to the mountainside above the Nau Swan, which ran parallel with the Wanasgul. Near the top of this pass, one of the ponies had a nasty fall; we unloaded both animals and led them slowly down through a jumbled mass of rocks for about half a mile on the other side. Coming down from the pass, I carried a light but ill-balanced load over this rough going, made more treacherous by the failing light.

We camped beside a large rock, on a patch of level ground at about 16,000 feet. There was no firewood, and very little water, but Zeman managed to brew some tea over a small fire of solidified paraffin. Abd al Nawab and the others had shared some bread, but I had eaten nothing since the previous night, and had been on the go all day searching for possible tracks. At this altitude it felt bitterly cold, and at intervals during the night I heard avalanches falling from a snow-plastered precipice nearby.

On 21 August we rose early to allow my companions enough time to cook some bread – a slow business using solid fuel – then spent the whole morning looking for a way of getting the ponies down through the sea of boulders to the valley bottom. But this proved to be a hopeless task.

I sent the ponies back, unloaded, with Abd al Nawab, Aiyub and the two ponymen to the ailoq in the Wanasgul, telling Abd al Nawab to try and engage porters when he got there. We put up the bivvy tent and, with enough solid paraffin for our requirements, we were quite snug.

Aiyub and the two Nuristani ponymen turned up at about 8.30 A M the following day, to take us and our baggage back down to the ailoq; and this time I managed a 40-pound load without any effort, although the going was still very bad.

I found Abd al Nawab, very alarmed, waiting for me at the ailoq. One of the shepherds had told him that, a few hours after we left there, on 20 August, six brothers from the Ramgul, well-known brigands armed with rifles, who had followed us from Puchal, had arrived at the ailoq and made enquiries about us. They said they would not molest us in Ramgul territory, but were planning to ambush us on the Kantiwar side of the pass, as they were on bad terms with that tribe. I was sceptical about this story which had put the wind right up Abd al Nawab.

Meanwhile, Abd al Nawab had found out that there was an easy pass from the ailoq into the Kulam valley. The next morning, at first light, I tried but failed to persuade our ponymen to take the Kulam Pass; but Abd al Nawab did not want to go this way for fear of meeting the brigands, and the ponymen, who refused to attempt any more passes, insisted on going back to Puchal. While we were discussing this, the owners of the ailoq insisted that they did not care where we went, but that we must leave at once, since our presence in the ailoq endangered them as the six brigands might come back at any moment. Their plea lent colour to the brigand story. As usual on journeys in these parts I was unarmed; besides, the two ponies had been very knocked about and one was lame from a badly fitting shoe which we could not get off. We decided therefore to return once more to Puchal.

On the way down the Wanasgul valley, our ponymen suddenly halted and demanded their wages. I refused to pay them until we had reached Puchal, otherwise they might have stopped for the night short of our destination. They went on, eventually, after an angry argument.

We had just arrived opposite Puchal when a mullah came down from the village, crossed over the bridge towards us and cursed us; he told us that we were to leave his country and never come back. Such people as were about certainly did not side with the mullah, but came up to us and shook hands. One of these bystanders, a Pathan, told him off and then took us with him to his house for the night.

The last few days had certainly been eventful: brigands, recalcitrant ponymen and, last but not least, a fanatical mullah.

I paid off our ponymen and engaged four Nuristani porters to carry our loads over the Purdam Pass to Kulam. The porters each demanded 100 Afghanis, which was about four times the going rate, but we were in their hands. They carried magnificently, however, and we reached Kulam in one day from Puchal.

We set off at 7.30 A M and marched rapidly down the valley to Lustagam. From here, the 6,000-foot climb up the steep mountainside opposite Lustagam was bloody; a continuous grind for almost six hours, with no let-up, over blocks of black basalt and the rocky moraine of an old glacier. The mountain here seemed unusually dry and desiccated: I saw no sign of water anywhere until we were near the summit, where a trickle seeping through the moraine gradually developed into a decent stream.

On a high grassy meadow just below the pass, we stopped for a short rest at an ailoq, where some shepherd-boys gave us a bowl of delicious buttermilk to drink. The mountains in this country were usually ridge-backed, and this was the only place where I saw a plateau. There were excellent grazing grounds up here, used by the Kulam tribe. Elsewhere the ailoqs were mostly in the villages and the animals grazed on the steep mountainsides. There had been hostilities between the Ramgul and Kantiwar tribes, due to a dispute about another, similar, plateau grazing ground.

Judging by the types of vegetation nearby, I guessed the altitude of the Purdam Pass was about 14,000 feet. From the top of the pass, I saw Mir Samir towering in the north-west; while, to the east, there was a tremendous view across one of the wildest tangles of gorges and precipices I have ever seen. Quite different to the Puchal side of the mountain, this harsh terrain, thrown together in apparently hopeless confusion, was more like the country I had expected to find in Nuristan.

The descent into the Kulam valley was very steep, past a big side-valley, the Steki, which came in from the right. I felt thankful that, instead of climbing up it, we were going down it to Kulam, where we arrived shortly before sunset, ten and a half hours after leaving Puchal.

Kulam village, the largest in this valley, consisted of about twenty houses, built on a spur at the junction of two valleys, with superb views in both directions. It must have had the finest situation of any village anywhere. There were fields and cultivations in the Steki valley and in the valley below Kulam; and the lower slopes of the surrounding mountains were forested with fir and junipers, as well as blue pines.

We spent two days here. The villagers gave us a house to stay in and everyone, including the agreeable old headman, was friendly. I took a number of photographs and spent the second evening collecting more plants for the British Museum; after dinner, the villagers sang and danced to tunes played on reed pipes and a viol. One boy, a Pathan from Logar, whose family had been exiled here, played the viol exceptionally well.

Kandaris moving down from Lake Shiva towards Faizabad in Badakhshan.

Above: Kandaris migrating from Lake Shiva.   Below: Kandaris on their migration.

Above: A Kandari.

Above: A young Shiah Tajik, at Miyan Deh in Munjan, carrying the fodder which he has gathered.

Below: A Gujur encampment in Munjan.

Below: A boy in the Parun valley.

Above: The Chamar Pass with the curious snow formations known as *névés pénitents*.

Below: A view from Mum.

The summit of Mir Samir from the Chamar Pass.

Above: My tent on the Derai Shuk side of the pass between Derai Shuk and Kantiwar.

Below: Pashki village, in the Parun valley.

Above: My Tajik
porters on the
Nuristan side of
the Chamar Pass.

Right: Ramgul,
Nuristanis at their
ailoq with skins
filled with butter.

Above: Chaman, in the Kantiwar valley.   Below: Kandari encampments.

My Safi porters from Kamdesh.

Above: My Safi porters cooking a meal.   Below: Kandaris near Balkh.

Right: Wood carvings on houses at Burg-i-Matral.

Below: Wama.

Below: Ladakh – villagers. Right: Chortens at Hemis monastery, near Leh.

Seated woman.

Seated man.

Previous page: The Annapurna range, Nepal. 'This
was the vision I took away with me from the Himalayas.'

Above: Nerags, near the Zanskar river.

The father of Sultan Muhammad, one of our porters, lived in this village, but he produced nothing for us except a few tomatoes. Sultan Muhammad had been one of the men I met at the ailoq in the Wanasgul, on 19 August, and it was he who had warned Abd al Nawab of the brigands.

Next morning we set off at dawn and marched all day as far as Piar, at the junction of the Kulam and Ramgul valleys. Between Gishkua and Almi, where the Shuk valley branched eastwards to Kantiwar, the river descended rapidly in a series of small cascades. The clouds of midges here were very bad indeed; they drew blood and their bites itched endlessly afterwards.

Some miles further down the valley, beyond Palagal, Sultan Muhammad and Aiyub put down their loads near a house and started trying to get more money out of us. Their exorbitant demands led to endless arguments – by now my enthusiasm for Nuristanis was wearing thin – which was a pity, for it left me eventually with a poor impression of them. The owner of the house, a bloody old man, could not resist giving his views on the porters' pay. He produced some curds, butter and bread, all dirty, and for these he charged us thirty Afghanis. The old man then tried to make us spend the night here and pay him for an extra day. Later, in my diary, I noted: 'NEVER travel in Nuristan dependent on local transport. The locals will unscrupulously exploit you. Use porters, not horses and bring them from Panjshir.'

For the last five miles, until we reached Piar, we followed a twisting track along the river which now flowed through an impressive narrow gorge between sheer-sided, smooth walls of rock, 300 feet high. This track would have been impossible for animal transport; we had to cross the river repeatedly over tree trunks which the locals had thrown across it, or by wading, in places nearly waist-deep, through the warm, fast-running water. Here, one of the porters picked up a branch of wild olive.

The gorge ended near Piar, a pleasant place where the Kulam and Ramgul valleys met. We camped for the night under a wild fig tree, on a small terrace immediately above the river. We were now in Pashaie country, and I was relieved to be no longer in the hands of Nuristanis.

The following morning Sultan Muhammad went back, and I engaged a Pashaie porter as his replacement. The Pashaie were originally Kafirs, but had been converted by Abd er Rahman shortly before he conquered Ramgul and the rest of Kafiristan. Below the convergence of the two valleys the hillside was covered with small piles of stones, commemorating the Muslims of Abd er Rahman's army who had been killed in battle here by the Kafirs.

We left Piar at sunrise, and after marching for about an hour, turned west up a narrow, twisting side-valley. Early that afternoon we arrived at Junia, the government headquarters for Nuristan and the first such post I had met with on this journey. Junia had an attractive setting, but could not have been more out of the way, stuck up this valley on the wrong side of a mountain range, and cut off by two very difficult valleys, the bottom ends of the Ramgul and Kulam, both almost impassable for anything but men on foot. The village houses were built in a style quite different from other houses in Nuristan; they were better constructed and the outer walls were given a plaster finish. Their most distinctive feature was a fringe of cut grass, held down by stones, which bordered the top of the parapet on the roofs, to run off the rain.

We were well received by the government officials in Junia.

Here I made a clean sweep of our porters, including Zeman, the cook, who of late had never stopped grumbling. I was glad to be rid of them.

We meant to get off in the afternoon, but after lunch it thundered and came on to rain, so we stayed where we were.

The following morning, our Pashaie porters turned up very late. We left Junia at 9.15 A M and marched straight up across the mountainside, through forests of oak and pine, to the Gapa Pass. The Pashaie ate the seeds from these pine-cones, and in some places the trees had been tapped for gum. We arrived at the top of the 11,000-foot pass at eleven, and rested there until midday.

A steep descent through more forests of oak and pine brought us to Korgal, an isolated village attractively situated on a small spur, with a fine view southwards down the valley.

The country here bore a striking resemblance to the Black Kafir valleys I had seen in Chitral. Walnut trees and small terraced fields of maize grew along the stream which flowed east from Korgal down to the Alingar river. I heard woodpeckers drumming among the trees. In the maize fields I noticed an ingenious device for scaring bears, which were common and did much damage to the crops, especially the maize: a small wheel was turned by the water in the stream, and this revolved an upright stick to which two arms were fastened. These arms hit a board and made a loud and continual noise.

The Pashaie villagers were exceptionally friendly. In Korgal we were put up in a house with a carved entrance door and carved pillars inside. The room we were given, which was clean, tidy and floored with a covering of fine grass, turned out to be the local mosque. This would certainly never have happened anywhere else in Nuristan. Our host was the mullah, a

Pathan gone Pashaie, who had the face of an elderly satyr with painted eyes and a bunch of herbs in his cap. He could not have been kinder or more helpful.

These Pashaie were quite different from the Nuristanis, being darker in colour, gentler in appearance and speaking a language of their own. They certainly appeared to be a different race. They painted their eyelids with a red stain, and sometimes even their eyebrows, which gave them an odd appearance; the young men and boys wore necklaces of beads, and put flowers in their caps and frequently carried small bunches of flowers in their hands. Many of them had flat metal ornaments in their ears, and most of the younger men were naked from the waist up, although a few of them wore goatskins across their shoulders; some wore skull caps or turbans, others Nuristani caps. The women were not in the least shy.

Ibex were to be found in many of the nearby mountains and markhor in others, especially the more forested ones. Here, in Korgal, I saw a good pair of markhor horns on the wall of a house.

The first of September was an exasperating day. It began with an argument when our porters tried to bargain more pay, but in the end they took an extra porter with them at their own expense, an old man who crawled along and stopped frequently to rest.

We set off at about seven and crossed a shoulder of the mountain, with the Alingar river flowing through a gorge below us; from here we descended, climbing with difficulty down over some very polished rock, to the mouth of the Shama valley. We then followed the Alingar for a short distance, before turning south-west up the Pashagar valley. The walk up this valley would have seemed rather attractive if I had not been so fed up with the porters. We had to keep pushing them along all day, and by the evening, having arrived at Pashagar village, I felt exhausted and irritable.

The village was built on a steep hillside, with narrow passageways between the houses, some of which had wooden balconies. We stayed in a well-built house with the village headman, who was accommodating but not hospitable. He refused to provide any bread, and devoured all the rice belonging to Abd al Qaiyun, one of our porters.

The noise of drums, pipes and singing in Somodar, a nearby village, opposite Pashagar, kept me awake until well after midnight.

From Pashagar we marched up the valley past Namka village, and then up a steep mountainside to the Wadau Pass. The lower slopes were covered with oak forests and, higher up, with two sorts of pine – the edible pine, and another non-edible variety with long thin cones. There were some fine, large pine trees near the pass where I arrived at 9 AM, an hour ahead of the porters.

The descent from the pass was very steep and took us two hours. About midday we reached Wadau which looked more primitive than the other Pashaie villages we had visited, and consisted of two groups of houses separated by a deepish valley filled with fruit trees. Everyone in Wadau was friendly and pleasant. We camped for the night on a small level patch of the hillside, near the mosque. After a few rumbles of thunder in the evening, the villagers told us that if it rained we should sleep inside the mosque.

The next day we set off again at 5.30 AM and rejoined the Alingar valley below Nangarag. We were now out of the hills and down in the valley plain. Coming along the west bank of the river, we passed a succession of villages – Lauqat, Kashkarai, Adar and Kundurwa among them. As we went further south the valley became wider, and the mountains had now receded several miles back on either side. Plantations of maize and beans and very green fields of rice grew along both banks of the river.

At Shahi, the district headquarters, I declined the offer of a very ungracious local official of a dark, dirty room near the shai khana. We were now among the Pathans; we exchanged our Pashaie porters for three young Pathans, and carried on as far as Barak Khan Baba, the site of a shrine.

The spacious Alingar valley was cultivated extensively with rice, maize and other crops, as well as orchards, with scattered forts of the usual Pathan type which had either square- or round-shaped towers at the corners. It had rained earlier, as we were coming down the valley, and the evening sunlight produced some very striking effects on the blue- and purple-shaded mountains.

On 4 September we started while it was still dark, and kept to the west bank of the river; we crossed the streams coming from two small side-valleys, and shortly before 8 A M we arrived at Kalatussiraj, the headquarters of Laghman, with its modern government buildings, and a ruined palace set in a pleasure garden. We paid off our three Pathan porters and, after an early lunch, I set off with Abd al Nawab in a horse-drawn tonga some twenty miles south-west from Kalatussiraj to Jalalabad.

At Chaharbagh we changed tongas, after a tyre had kept coming off, the harness had broken and the horses seemed to be on the point of collapsing. The next driver knocked his horses about unmercifully, hitting them over their heads until they refused to go on; but, despite these frustrating delays, we eventually reached Jalalabad before dark.

We spent three nights in the hotel at Jalalabad, followed by two more nights in Peshawar. From Peshawar I travelled by train to Karachi and, from there, I flew back to Basra.

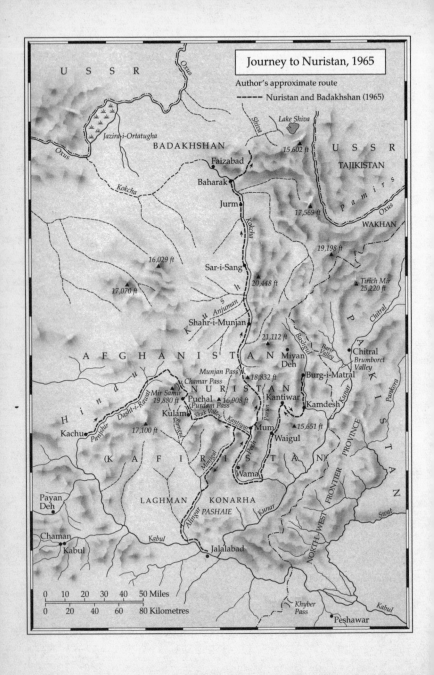

Journey to Nuristan, 1965

Author's approximate route
- - - Nuristan and Badakhshan (1965)

U S S R

Oxus

Jazira-i-Ortatugha

BADAKHSHAN

Oxus

Kokcha

Shiva

Lake Shiva

15,602 ft

U S S R

TAJIKISTAN

Faizabad

Baharak

Jurm

Kokcha

Pamirs

17,569 ft

Oxus

WAKHAN

19,198 ft

Sar-i-Sang

16,029 ft

17,070 ft

20,448 ft

Tirich Mir
25,220 ft

K   u   s   h

Anjuman

Shahr-i-Munjan

A F G H A N I S T A N

21,112 ft

Miyan
Deh

Bashgul

Harki
Valley

Chitral

Chitral

Brumboret
Valley

Munjan Pass

Chamar Pass

Mir Samir
19,880 ft

Puchal

18,832 ft

N U R I S T A N

Burg-i-Matral

Kamdesh

Parun

H   i   n   d   u

Dasht-i-Rawat

Purdam Pass

16,908 ft

Kantiwar

Kunar

Kulam

Shuk Valley

Kantiwar

Kachu

Parandtir

Ramgul

17,100 ft

(K   A   F   I   R   I   S

Minjani

Mum

Waigul

15,651 ft

T   A   N)

P
R
O
V
I
N
C
E

Kamdesh

N
O
R
T
H
-
W
E
S
T

F
R
O
N
T
I
E
R

K
I
S
T
A
N

Payan
Deh

LAGHMAN

KONARHA

Wama

Alingar

PASHAIE

Kunar

Swat

Chaman

Kabul

Kabul

Jalalabad

Pankora

0   10   20   30   40   50 Miles

0   20   40   60   80 Kilometres

Khyber
Pass

Kabul

Peshawar

NURISTAN II
1965

IT WAS NINE YEARS before I returned to Nuristan, in 1965. The intervening years had been eventful ones. After I returned to England from the Iraqi Marshes at the end of 1956, I devoted most of 1957 to writing my first book, *Arabian Sands*; the following year I again spent six months in the Marshes, but this chapter in my life closed after the revolution in Baghdad in 1958. During 1959 and 1960, I travelled extensively with mules in Ethiopia. From 1960 to 1963, I journeyed on foot, with camels or donkeys, all over the former Northern Frontier District of Kenya and northern Tanzania, except for an interlude, 1961–62, when I wrote *The Marsh Arabs*. In 1964, in Iran, I travelled in the Elburz Mountains, then I joined the Bakhtiari nomads on their annual migration through the Zagros mountains, and afterwards crossed the Dasht-i-Lut.

I now wished to see more of Nuristan than I had seen on my previous journey, which had lasted only five weeks. I flew from Teheran to Karachi and arrived on 16 June 1965 at Kabul, where I stayed with the British Consul, Nancy Clay. A week later I left Kabul, accompanied by an Afghan student, Baz Muhammad, as my interpreter, and drove in a British Embassy Land-Rover up the Panjshir valley to Dasht-i-Rawat.

For the next two days we travelled north-west up the Panjshir to its junction with the Chamar valley. I intended to cross again by the Chamar Pass into Nuristan and travel in areas I had not been able to visit during my previous journey in 1956.

On Thursday 24 June, I set off with Baz Muhammad and six Tajik porters. We marched upstream along the west bank of the Panjshir river, and at midday camped beside the river opposite an ailoq.

The next day was hot. We continued on past the Khawak and Arayu side-valleys, and spent the night at Qalat-i-Parian, where the villagers fed us with mutton from a freshly-killed sheep.

The following morning, 26 June, we were given breakfast in Kaujan at a house with attractive double yellow, single pink and white roses in full bloom nearby. A little way beyond Gishta, we crossed the river by a bridge. At the next village, Char-i-Balan, we rested to eat curds; then we turned east up the Chamar, where small black cattle grazed amid scenery dominated by the snow mountains at either end of the valley.

The next morning we started early and marched on up the Chamar valley past several ailoqs, where the shepherds gave us curds and cheese; on the way, I noticed a pair of immature lammergeyers and the porters saw an ibex in the distance. At midday we camped in a deserted ailoq, the highest in the valley. The patches of green turf nearby were covered with small, pale-lavender-coloured primulas. Dry dung from the floor of a sheep-pen provided us with fuel.

The snow-capped shoulder of Mir Samir towered high above our camp, and all round us, especially at the upper end of the valley, the mountainsides were white with snow. Clouds gathered in the evening.

*

It was still dark the following day when we started off up the valley towards the pass. At sunrise we passed one of my old camping-sites. Beyond this we trudged uphill with great difficulty through snow which was knee-deep. Higher up on the northern face, the snow had been eroded into frozen pinnacles, two feet high and a foot or so apart, the formation known to mountaineers as *névés pénitents*, laborious to cross.

At midday we finally reached the top of the pass. The atmosphere was very clear and I took some photographs of Mir Samir, its snow-capped summit rising in the south-west, less than 4,000 feet above us. On the south face, below the pass, the snow was soft and in places about three feet deep. We squatted on our heels and glissaded down to the Ramgul valley, sliding our heavy 60–70 pound loads along with us.

The porters had carried well, but were tired by the time we got to the valley bottom, away from the snow, and camped for the night in an empty ailoq.

We set off down the valley next morning, marching on green turf scattered with primulas and other tiny yellow flowers. Snow covered the lower slopes on either side of the valley; the Chamar stream flowed very fast and clear, and we could hear the sound of water everywhere.

An hour or so later we stopped at an ailoq, where some Nuristani shepherds gave us milk and curds. Among them was the Nuristani who, on the last journey, had tried to kill my Tajik ponyman; he was very friendly as indeed were the others, and insisted that we should camp beside the ailoq.

Later that day, I put my back out coughing. At first, next morning, I was barely able to walk, but gradually my back got easier. We went slowly on down the valley, past another ailoq, where I noticed a small single yellow rose and some yellow asphodel. High up on the snow-covered mountainside I saw a bear.

We started at 7.15 A M on 1 July and crossed the river five times, where it flowed through an impressive gorge, near its junction with the Mangashir. At Atati, a hillside village where we rested briefly, I found more roses in bloom. We then marched on from Atati for two hours, and arrived soon after 3 P M at Puchal where we put up the tent beneath some mulberry trees.

We spent the whole of the next day at Puchal. Unlike my previous visits, this time everyone in the village including the mullahs – even the mullah who had cursed me – was welcoming and friendly.

Throughout this journey I remained on good terms with the Nuristanis. Unlike Robertson, I never had anything stolen by them, nor did I find them avaricious. They would drive a hard bargain, but many of them, especially in villages unused to Europeans, were exceedingly hospitable.

We left the main village an hour after sunrise, heading for Kulam. A little further downstream, we stopped at the smaller group of a dozen dwellings forming lower Puchal, where I had stayed in 1956. We then crossed the river by the bridge and climbed for two hours up the mountainside. Higher up the mountain, there was no sign of water until we reached an ailoq surrounded by drifts of snow.

That evening two Tajiks turned up, and they and the porters bought a goat from the owner of the ailoq. They ate it all, after giving Baz Muhammad and me as much meat as we wanted. After dinner, two Nuristani herd-boys sang and so did one of the Tajiks.

At dawn a thick blanket of low cloud hid the mountains. We set off just as it was getting light, and climbed to the top of the Purdam Pass. The way up involved a steady slog for three hours over hard snow, scree and boulders, and the descent from the pass was very steep, but we found hardly any snow lying on the Kulam side except in the gullies. Further down, we came to an ailoq built of tree-trunks. Thick forests covered the lower slopes, with water everywhere and green grass strewn with pink asphodels and other flowers beneath the trees which included some magnificent large junipers and pines.

We halted at a village on a spur above the confluence of two rivers, the Goulata, also known as the Purdam, and the Bedetsau. The villager who put us up for the night had recently killed his wife and her lover, a man from across the valley. The ensuing blood-feud between our host's family and the family of the dead man had already resulted in some shooting the day before, and reinforcements turned up soon after we got here.

I found these people very hospitable. They gave us lunch as soon as we arrived, then dinner; and the following morning they gave us a very good breakfast. As we were leaving, the villagers became very excited, having spotted our host's enemies on the mountainside opposite.

The local chief, Habib Allah Khan, who stood six foot four, invited us to stay at his house further down the river. From midday, when we arrived there, until the late evening he left us with nothing to eat; in consequence everyone felt browned off. Instead, the wretched man spent his time trying to make me give him my wrist-watch.

Next morning we set off at daybreak and marched downstream for three hours to the junction with Derai Shuk, a big river-valley with a pass at the head of it which led into Kantiwar.

We crossed the river and went on east up the Shuk valley as far as Taurich, a small village high up on the mountainside. Here occurred the only real disagreement I ever had with the Nuristanis. The people gave us food on our arrival; we gorged on mulberries with bread and curds. Unwilling to impose eight of us on them again in the evening, I bought with difficulty a chicken which we cooked and ate with some boiled rice for dinner. This gave great offence: although we had camped on a roof instead of sleeping in someone's house, the furious villagers maintained we were their guests and said we had scorned their hospitality.

The villagers refused to see us off the following morning. We left Taurich at 6 A M and marched up the valley for two hours until we reached Shuk, an attractive village clinging to the mountainside, where we rested under some trees by the mosque. All the villagers, including the mullah, were very friendly. In the afternoon we moved the loads to a nearby roof and set up the tent beside them. The views from here up and down the valley were magnificent, among the finest I have ever seen. Nuristan was a land of great contrasts, reminding me sometimes of Kurdistan but on a vaster scale. Across the river, forests of holly-oak covered the steep mountainsides; pine trees grew higher up on the ridges, and all round us the mountain peaks glistened white with snow.

Some bundles of wheat cut by the women had been spread on another roof, and children romped in the wheat to thresh it. In Nuristan, only men and boys went up to the ailoqs and only the women and girls worked in the fields.

Four hours later we reached the top of the pass overlooking Kantiwar. The climb over hard snow had been steady, but relatively easy. On the far side of the mountain, we descended from the pass through deep, soft snow until we came to an empty ailoq on a patch of turf scattered with flowers. We rested here, and rested again at another empty ailoq lower down, where we made tea over a fire of dry dung.

The way from here, down the face of the mountain to the valley floor, was steep and difficult. The scenery was magnificent: snow-covered mountains; a deep gorge with a racing river, and high up in the valley, flocks of sheep and goats tended by Gujurs.

Massive drifts of snow lay in the valley bottom. We crossed the icy torrent on a snow bridge and camped in the shelter of some rocks; the bushes nearby provided us with firewood. Huddled round the fire under a full moon, the porters worried that we might have been followed by Gujur bandits.

The following morning we marched down the valley through a wood of large birch trees and willows, then across open grassy meadows intersected by streams. After about an hour, we stopped beside a Nuristani ailoq. The shepherds in the ailoq welcomed us; one of them said that they had been asked not to kill strangers.

We pitched the tent close to the river which was wider here, slow-flowing and very clear. Known as Chaman, this was a delectable place where the untroubled water idled past, dragging at the overhanging willow in the current; where black cattle, watched by boys with flutes, grazed on rich pasture among banks of lilac primulas, wild roses, purple orchids, asphodel and grass of Parnassus.

From Chaman we now descended through a narrow stretch of the Kantiwar valley, between overshadowing precipitous mountainsides clothed with pine and juniper. In places the water hurled itself against the cliffs and our only way was up notched tree-trunks placed against the polished rocks.

Towards noon, we arrived at Debola, a large cluster of houses among mulberry trees on a gently sloping hillside above a fairly broad, cultivated plain; well sited at the junction of the Kantiwar and Parun valleys, the village was dominated by a rectangular fort whose owner, a general, had died some time ago.

We spent the following day at Debola lazing in the sun among a mass of wild flowers. There was a school here for training mullahs, and some very good-looking young students came and sat with us, looking incongruously like dancing-boys with their long hair and painted eyes. These boys, and a few of the village elders, wanted to be photographed. I also took photographs of several carved wooden butter measures, and cooking-pots with spouts and handles made of stone.

We left early the next morning and continued down the valley past Payandeh, along a narrow, uncultivated gorge; we then climbed through forests of holly-oak and pine over a very steep shoulder of the mountain, to Mum on the massive promontory overlooking the confluence of the Kantiwar and Parun rivers.

Mum was a small village in a forest of huge deodars, about twenty houses surrounded by bushes covered with pink flowers. We reached the village hot and exhausted after a long, stiff scramble, but cloud swirled among the cedars, intermittently shutting out the valley, and we were soon chilled; the villagers lit a fire, gave us food and were very friendly.

The following morning, at sunrise, we left Mum and climbed gradually for two hours through cedar woods which reached as high as the next pass. From the top of the pass we descended by a steep track through magnificent forests of cedar and pine to the bottom of Parun valley.

We spent the night at Pashki, a large village of a hundred houses, on the hillside above the fields. Here the valley widened out and every scrap of level ground was cultivated. Women toiled all day in these cultivated places, strips of wheat, maize or millet; or tended little vegetable patches.

We continued our journey the following morning at 6.45 A M and marched up the Parun river, with a high range of snow mountains ahead of us. Poplars, walnuts and willows grew along the river bank, and a large tree with a double nut, which I could not identify. As the valley became narrower we passed more villages and cultivations before we halted for a meal at Kushtakeh; near this village I saw the site of a temple dedicated to Imra, one of the Kafir gods.

An hour's march from Kushtakeh brought us to Dewah, where a bridge over the Parun connected the groups of houses built on opposite sides of the river. The villagers in Dewah wore long or short coats and breeches, which they bound round their calves with tape. The coats and breeches were made from a white cloth like corduroy and decorated with patterns coloured in red or purple.

As we came along the valley I noticed masses of purple orchids growing wherever a strip of marshy ground bordered a stream. We passed a village, the name of which sounded to me like Parunz, or possibly Prontz, and at 10.30 A M we arrived at Eshtawi. We camped here under some trees above the village. Eshtawi, like Dewah, was divided in two parts; in the lower village there were more houses, a watch-tower, and a mosque with a carved wooden lintel over the door.

*

I was keen to visit Lake Shiva in Badakhshan, where in summer the nomad Pathans, known locally as Kandaris, congregated. The way north from here to Badakhshan involved a steep trek up a side-valley over the Munjan Pass, out of Nuristan. We had been warned of deep snow, and four Nuristanis from the village came with us to help carry our loads as far as the top of the pass. We marched for three hours, and camped at an empty ailoq, just below the snow-line, where we met a party of twelve Munjanis carrying salt down to Parun. Soon after we arrived at the ailoq, showers of rain mixed with hail started to fall. These cleared away by the evening, during the night a storm of thunder and lightning broke over the mountains to the west, but we had no more rain.

We set off next morning at first light and climbed up the steep, snow-covered mountainside to the top of the Munjan Pass. Near the pass we noticed the tracks of a snow leopard. An icy wind blew as we slowly picked our way over ridges and pinnacles of hard-frozen snow and the same *névés pénitents* formation we had found when crossing the Chamar Pass three weeks previously.

The four Nuristanis went back from here to their village. We had an easy descent, still on hard snow, past several small blue-green tarns; then we came to grassy flats carpeted with lilac primulas, where we rested by a lake. Two more parties of Munjanis laden with rock salt passed us on the way.

Lower down, below the bare, scree-covered mountainsides, flocks of sheep and goats tended by Gujurs grazed on well-watered pastures among beautiful violet cranesbill and grass of Parnassus. We camped beside the river, near a bed of stunted willows. Snow lay here in deep drifts at the head of the valley; it became bitterly cold by sunset, but we collected plenty of wood and had a good fire.

Next morning we stopped at a Gujur encampment where they gave us hot milk to drink. Then we carried on down the valley, between high rocky mountains streaked with snow, past the intersection with another big valley coming from the Kantiwar Pass. We crossed the river near its confluence and camped at Naw-i-Munjan, a small village of less than a dozen houses, where I found wild roses and lavender growing alongside cultivations of lucerne. The men in this village were Nuristanis from Waigul who had married Tajik women.

We spent the following morning here to rest the porters. We started at 1.30 PM and marched due north along the river. This stretch of the valley was much wider, and here the river flowed over a broad bed of shingle, its banks edged with willows, poplars and pink or white roses.

After three hours we reached Tili, a poor village where all the houses were covered by a contiguous flat roof decorated with a few ibex horns. During the night an earth tremor shook the village. All the villagers immediately evacuated their houses, but perhaps due to gusts of wind buffeting the tent neither Baz Muhammad nor I felt the tremor and went on sleeping.

Keeping to the east bank of the river, a few miles beyond Tili we passed a large ruined castle, known as Qalat-i-Shah, the residence of an important Sayid. We halted further on at Miyan Deh and camped beside the river. The Sayid who owned the castle had been away, but he turned up later in our camp. Wearing a Nuristani cap instead of a turban, he was a striking-looking man and very agreeable. The local people called him the Shah.

We spent the following day at Miyan Deh in order to buy flour. Eventually we got two seers, roughly equivalent to five pounds, and the porters used most of it in the evening. There was almost nothing else to be had in this village, not even firewood.

To pass the time I took some photographs of children.

During the day a Nuristani from Waigul turned up. The Munjanis, who were Shiah Tajiks, feared the Nuristanis; this man was a notorious brigand and horse-thief and his arrival put the entire village in a flap.

I was glad to get away from there next morning. The valley beyond Miyan Deh was bare, but later we passed a number of small villages and fields. We passed some grazing yaks, where the high mountains on either side rose above a small lake set in a wide plain. After this we crossed a fair-sized river, which flowed into the main valley from the east, and we reached Shahr-i-Munjan by mid-afternoon. This village of some two hundred houses was the largest I had yet seen. The ruler of Munjan happened to be staying here and I complained to him about the Nuristani brigand who had followed us all morning from Miyan Deh as far as Vilo.

Here I saw a pillar, probably some kind of memorial, built of stones and surmounted by a fine markhor head; there were ruins on a rock above the village.

Next morning we forded a river which flowed eastwards from Sanglich into the Kokcha valley above Shahr-i-Munjan. From here we crossed over a bare, desolate shoulder of the mountain. Coming down the far side I met Nicholas Downay, an adventurous young friend of mine, accompanied by four porters, heading for Parun; a few months previously, in England, he had told me that he was planning to travel in Nuristan. He looked very fit, confident, happy and very much in charge. Now we sat and talked in a biting wind on the mountainside until our shivering porters insisted that we went our separate ways.

An uncle of the shah from Miyan Deh gave us bread and tea in his house at Rabat which reminded me of a typical Chitrali house; then we marched on to Sekwaou, where we camped in a pleasant courtyard. Some government officials were also staying here; except for them, everyone in this friendly village had heard of the Nuristani brigand and I felt a little concerned about Nicholas crossing the Munjan Pass.

Next day, a little way above Sekwaou, we had to cross a stretch of the Munjan river which was waist-deep in places and very fast-flowing. We hired a pony to carry the loads, and one of the villagers, a brother of my Tajik porter, Ghulam Zubair, lent us another. It took about three hours to get our loads across the river. Baz Muhammad's pony, carrying our food, foundered in a quicksand beside the river but by a miracle only the onions got wet. Later my pony came down with me; it fell on my leg, but I managed to keep my camera dry.

The following morning, after a long delay, we bought some flour and set off down the Munjan river towards its junction with Anjuman. Two Germans had been murdered there the previous year. On a spur above the river were the ruins of a castle reputedly built by Hulagu, a grandson of Genghis Khan. Near the village of Iskajar another of Hulagu's castles lay in ruins, and beyond this the remains of ancient terraced cultivations also said to be of Mongol origin. We camped beside a house in Iskajar and, through Baz Muhammad, I asked our host to cook for us what was left of our mutton. He did so, but his son ate my portion on his way to the tent, leaving me with nothing to eat except a few apricots.

*

Next morning I found many drawings of ibex, which must have been centuries old, and some more recent Arabic inscriptions, on rock-faces near the river junction. From there we climbed up to the promontory where I saw the ruins of Hulagu's small castle, its slit windows still visible in the debris of mud-plastered, rough stone walls.

Baz Muhammad had hurt his knee as a result of his fall in the quicksands. To rest his leg we lingered by the river and drank tea among flowering tamarisk and strands of willow, until the early afternoon; we then marched slowly as far as Parawa, and camped there for the night.

The sky gradually cleared during the morning as we marched down the valley to Sar-i-Sang, where lapis lazuli was still mined. All the lapis lazuli so extensively used in ancient Egypt, including the tomb artifacts of Tutankhamun, had come from this one valley in the remote mountains of Central Asia.

The officials in charge of the mine refused to allow my Panjshiri porters into their camp, so we sent them ahead to the next village, except for Ghulam Zubair, who remained with me. To reach the mine, we had to cross again to the east bank of the river. Here we saw whole cliff faces of flawless white marble, with huge blocks of marble scattered in the valley below them. All of the silicate which constitutes lapis lazuli was extracted from these white marble cliffs.

From here we marched on to Esposmi the next day.

The track from the mine to Esposmi led through a very impressive gorge where the river rushed along between steep banks of scree with sheer rock-faces rising above them. There was almost no vegetation in the gorge, even by the river, and to get round the cliffs we had to climb in a strong north wind over five small passes. Mountains flecked with snow towered high above the gorge on either side, and I could see massive snow peaks and snowfields further away at the head of the valley.

At Esposmi I paid off all our Tajik porters except Ghulam Zubair; from here the director of the mine sent ahead to Hazarat es Said for his jeep. The country opened out near this fairly large village, where we arrived after a further march of two hours just as it was getting dark.

In the morning we drove with the director up the valley to Jurm, where we called on the Governor of Badakhshan; from there we went on to Baharak. Beyond Jurm the valley widened and we passed cultivated fields and pastures, groves of poplars, and villages set about with orchards and inhabited by Tajiks and Uzbeks, who wore turbans and padded robes of many colours. Roses grew in the hedges.

The following evening we left Baharak, with two horses and two Uzbeks, and rode out over an empty plain to Formoragh.

At sunrise, we rode high up into the rolling sweep of bare mountains above the plain. I had hoped to find the Kandaris at their massed encampments beyond the pass above the Oxus valley, near Lake Shiva, but we were too late. These nomads arrived at Shiva at the end of May; now, at the beginning of August, they had already left the lake where, it was said, two hundred thousand of them congregated with their flocks. Down slopes that were almost colourless in the hazy light, but for the vagrant shadows of scattered clouds, there came winding towards us a continuous thread of men and camels. They followed no apparent course, turning, twisting, disappearing into hollows and reappearing. The weather was still broken after heavy rain the previous day which had brought the mountain streams crashing down in spate.

We dismounted and stood aside to let them pass: camels tied

head to tail, laden with tents, poles and the scanty furnishings and possessions of a nomad people; each camel decorated with tufted woollen head-stalls and wide tasselled neckbands; many with bells fastened above their knees; laden donkeys and horses; small children and a woman or two perched on the loads; women in voluminous clothes with black draperies over their heads, leading strings of camels; bearded men and smooth-faced youths striding past, in turbans, patterned waist-coats and long cloaks; and guard dogs padding by, formidable brutes that could kill a wolf. I had seen the great tribes of northern Arabia – the Bakhtiari of Persia, the Herki of Kurdistan, and the Powindah coming down to Pakistan – yet for some reason, perhaps the landscape, my memory of these Kandaris remains the most vivid of them all.

We spent the night camped with some Uzbeks near the pass and the following morning I took many photographs of the Kandaris as they streamed down towards the plains.

In Faizabad I hired a car to take Baz Muhammad, Ghulam Zubair and me back to Kabul. There, I paid off Baz Muhammad and engaged another interpreter called Kemal ed Din.

Ten days later, on 20 August, I left Kabul with Kemal ed Din and Ghulam Zubair, who had remained with me, and drove in a Land-Rover to Kamdesh by way of Jalalabad, Shaqa Sarai and Barikot. Kamdesh, at the southern end of the Bashgul valley, had recently been made accessible from Kabul by road, and it was now fashionable in the embassies to visit Nuristan by driving as far as Kamdesh.

After hiring five porters we left Kamdesh the following week and marched up the Bashgul valley. We stopped half-way between villages called Mindagul and Marwa, and ate lunch under some trees beside the rushing river. This narrow stretch of the valley was flanked by granite precipices which, to me, looked unclimbable. Coming along the valley we saw mulberry trees, walnuts, figs and some wild vines with grapes ripe enough to eat, but few crops apart from Indian corn.

The next day we started at 6.45 AM and marched as far as Tapu, where we rested for several hours under the walnut trees and cooked a meal. Another steady walk of three hours brought us to Burg-i-Matral. The track bordered the river, now a foaming torrent, which hurtled past in a continuous cascade. Holly-oaks and pines grew higher up on the steep mountainsides, and drifts of snow lay in the gorges to the right and left of us.

The mountainsides below Burg-i-Matral were less steep and rocky than those further down the valley. This large, very attractive village consisted of about two hundred houses and was divided in two parts, one on either side of the river, connected by a well-made bridge.

The following day, in Burg-i-Matral, I took many photographs of the houses and carvings which dated from the old Kafir days. Here the wooden facings on fronts and sides of houses were carved in intricately varied patterns, which included wheel-shaped motifs. In *The Kafirs of the Hindu Kush* Robertson had disparaged this woodwork: I thought it superb. That evening a blind mullah sang us songs.

Two days later we arrived back at Kamdesh. After a brief visit to the fort, we made a steep, hot climb up the mountainside to the village where we camped under a mulberry tree in a gap between the houses. No-one made the least effort to help us. We managed eventually to buy a chicken, and sent the five Safi porters back to their village for the night.

The porters returned to Kamdesh at first light. We climbed up to the ridge above the village, then came down through forests of pine and deodar into the Nichingal valley. We bought a seer of flour in Kustos, a village with a fine watch-tower. Further down the valley I had a good view eastward to the mountains of Chitral. That evening we camped under a jutting rock close to the river, and made a big, rather smoky fire of driftwood.

Next morning we marched for two hours along the Nichingal, then turned west up the Warara valley, heading for the pass into Waigul. Mud-slides and hard-packed drifts of snow lay in the cleft of this steep valley; tiny yellow primulas and long-stemmed white asphodel grew on the hillsides.

Further up the valley we bought a small goat from a herds-man who refused to disclose the whereabouts of his ailoq, and I thought, what a maddening crowd these Kamdesh people are.

We spent the night camped on the mountainside, with very little firewood; after dark we had a heavy storm of hail, followed by torrential rain and thunder.

The next day we approached the pass, above a snowfield, along a grassy hillside scattered with many kinds of wild flowers: minute gentians; pink primulas almost as small as the yellow ones I had seen the day before; tiny forget-me-nots and a glorious violet cranesbill.

The clouds had gathered early; as we were eating lunch beside a stream a hailstorm broke, followed by snow. It kept snowing all the way up to the pass, but it petered out soon after midday.

We descended in bright sunshine past some ailoqs down to a forest of pines and juniper. At the edge of the forest we found an empty, well-built cabin where we camped for the night.

That evening two of the porters had a row; one of them, who was armed with a revolver, threatened to shoot the other man while he was asleep. As a precaution I took his revolver away from him.

The Waigul valley was narrow but impressive, enclosed by high, bare precipices which rose above forests of deodar and pencil cedar; deodar became more common further down the valley. Here, on the lower slopes, the farmers irrigated their fields of millet with water carried across the river by aqueducts made from hollowed-out tree-trunks supported on ladders. Some houses I saw had tented roofs of poles overlaid with woven grass and branches, designed to shed the snow.

At a Gujur encampment, we were given freshly baked bread; we then marched for an hour, and camped at 1.30 PM at Etok village, in the shelter of a house built on stilts, just as it started to rain.

In the evening one of the villagers went up the mountain to try and shoot a markhor. He nicked a pregnant female which escaped unwounded, and brought back the small tuft of its hair cut by the bullet.

We left Etok at sunrise, and arrived four hours later in Waigul. Here the large village of some three hundred houses had been divided in two groups: upper Waigul, which clung to a pale limestone cliff, each jutting house propped on stilts and seeming as small as a swallow's nest, and lower Waigul, reached by a steep built-up path made of rocks spread on tree-trunks which led down the sheer cliff-face.

The supporting pillars inside the houses were elaborately carved, and many doors and sideposts were adorned with stylized patterns of ibex or markhor horns. Sometimes actual markhor horns flanked the entrance, the skulls of the animals set one above another, or they were used to decorate the outside walls. Some of these horns were larger than any I had seen in Rowland Ward's *Records of Big Game*. On one house there were sixteen heads, all shot by the owner.

Markhor heads were often placed against the carved wooden coffins of the dead; these were left in the open and sometimes we were sickened by the stench. It was as well that there were no hyenas or they would soon have tugged out the corpses. Frequently elaborately carved wooden ornaments had been set up near the coffins, but owing to the influence of Islam none of them now represented human figures.

Next morning we took the wrong track and got further and further from the pass into Ranchingal and Pech. Finally we worked our way across the mountainside by way of three deep and very steep gorges, and reached the top of the pass by the middle of the afternoon. In the Ranchingal valley, we found a peaceful spot among the pines and cedars and slept on the flat roof of a hut, long since deserted, with a small stream flowing through it.

The houses in Ranchingal village, like Waigul, were divided in two groups and built on stilts against a steep hillside. I photographed more markhor-horn decorations carved on doors and sideposts. We camped for the night on the roof of the mosque, and this I found very agreeable; but the people were unhelpful and charged fantastic prices for chickens, butter and flour.

We set off at 6.30 AM and marched for three miles down the valley, then along the mountainside some 400–700 feet above the river. Later, we camped in a side-valley below Muldesh village. This was a hot day, and we were much troubled by midges.

Compared to the western parts of Nuristan, the country here was less mullah-ridden. In Kamdesh and Waigul, the women were much freer; they did not scuttle off into the bushes as soon as they saw us, but walked past us with their faces uncovered and sometimes gave us a greeting.

From Muldesh we came down the mountainside and along the river to Wat, the last Nuristani village in Ranchingal. After this we passed several Pathan villages, where I saw men floating downriver heavy logs which they had felled and dragged down from the forested slopes above the valley. Beyond Nagalam we skirted some rice-fields and turned back north into Pech. In Manugai, at the junction of the Pech and Waigul rivers, we camped near a small government post. We spent the next day here, bought more flour and exchanged our porters for five others – all Safis – who were called Ali Dost, Said Khan, Nawab Khan, Gul Rahman and Dowlat Khan.

The Pech valley was well-populated here, with cultivations on both sides of the river and villages every half a mile or so along the track.

Near one of these villages, our porter, Ali Dost, had an incredibly lucky escape. We had stopped at 8 A M that morning beside a roadside mosque to make tea, and he had climbed a tree to cut branches for firewood. He slipped and fell thirty feet to the ground, narrowly missing the mosque's stone parapet. A branch broke his fall, but at first I thought he was dead, or at least seriously injured. After a rest, however, he seemed none the worse and marched on with us up the valley, while my interpreter carried his load.

Ali Dost had completely recovered by the time we camped

that evening under some big mulberry trees near a malik's house.

We travelled for the next four days up the Pech valley towards Kantiwar. All the way we passed villages and small fields of Indian corn, millet, pumpkins and beans. In Gosalak the villagers gave us pomegranates, and near here we met boys carrying bundles of grapes; elsewhere in this valley I saw figtrees, mulberries and wild olives. We did not bother to put up the tent at night, except once during a violent thunderstorm when it poured with rain.

On 9 September we arrived at Wama, a cluster of three separate villages in a superb position above a gorge. The houses were raised on stilts and adorned with some fine markhor horns.

We marched on the next day through spectacular scenery, between high sheer flanks of bare rock rising above forests inhabited by black bear; the water in the river was the clearest I had seen, coloured bottle-green in certain lights. In one place, we saw fish about the size of a small trout packed solid in a shallow backwater.

Below the junction of the Parun and Kantiwar rivers, we crossed to the west bank and went on up the narrow Kantiwar valley. We rested at Chaman until the early afternoon, and later camped directly below Mum where I had stayed on 16 July. It was cold that evening, but we set light to a fallen tree which gave us a good fire.

Beyond the enclosing forested slopes near Mum, the valley widened towards Payandeh. Here the villagers had recently rebuilt their mosque, and I found some finely-carved pillars from the old mosque lying under a tree. Payandeh was the furthest west in Nuristan I saw any good carving.

We spent the night at Debola, an hour's march from Payandeh, camped under some mulberry trees beside the village mosque. Four days earlier there had been fighting between the Debola villagers and the people of Chaman who came from Puchal. Four men from Debola had been killed, and eight from Chaman. When we arrived in Debola we found chiefs from Puchal in the village taking part in a feast to celebrate the peace.

The next day the malik's brother fell ill, with a high fever and stomach pains. I gave him antibiotics and he was better by the evening. I had successfully doctored some villagers when I visited Debola in July, and I now treated many others.

We left early and after a short distance began a steady climb up the valley of Gosht. On our way up the valley we met a man from Jalalabad who took us to a Gujur encampment, high above the tree-line, where we spent the night. His daughter had married one of the Gujurs.

Next day we lazed in the sun beneath a cloudless turquoise sky. An occasional lammergeyer circled above the camp, but here, as in other parts of Nuristan, there were surprisingly few birds to be seen. We bought a sheep and that evening, after dinner, the Gujurs played their flutes and sang as we sat together round the fire.

The following morning we set off at 6.30 towards the pass. A young dog from the Gujur camp came with us, and soon after we left he caught and killed a marmot.

At first the going was easy, but it became steep and tiring as we climbed higher on drifts of hard, frozen snow. Three hours later we reached the top of the pass where there was a plateau, strewn with deep blue gentians, and a small lake. All the porters complained of headaches, and Kemal ed Din was sick;

however, we had brought some firewood with us and the men felt better after a rest and a meal in this pleasant setting by the lake shore.

From the pass we had some difficulty deciding which way to go, but a gradual descent, followed by a steeper one over exposed rock, brought us to an abandoned Gujur settlement where we made camp. Later I heard that this settlement had been destroyed three weeks previously by Ashkun tribesmen from Minjigal. Rafters from the ruined mosque provided us with firewood, and the porters slept in the shelter of its walls.

The head of the valley was known as Ashkugal; after the abandoned Gujur settlement it became the Minjigal. Next morning we marched south-west down the valley, between forested slopes of scattered oak and pencil cedar, past another deserted settlement of more than thirty huts. The Ashkun, it appeared, had driven all the Gujurs out of this valley. Further down we came to yet another empty settlement at the foot of a smooth, sheer-sided granite cliff.

We met parties of Askhun the following day at two small encampments; the men armed with rifles were indeed a rough-looking lot. We bought a sheep from them, and cooked lunch at a nice sandy spot among some rocks by the river. When it began to rain heavily we moved the loads into a cave beneath a rocky overhang. A grave under a pile of rocks inside the cave, and many more rocks lying about on the cave floor, made our sleeping arrangements rather cramped; but no-one minded. The young Gujur dog was still with us, and guarded our camp very effectively at night.

Next day the track down the Minjigal valley took us high above the river, along narrow rocky ledges jutting from the sheer face of a precipitous gorge. In places, a built-up path of stones heaped on branches spanned the wide gaps between some of these ledges. During the morning I noticed three vultures, the first I had seen in Nuristan, circling above a peak. We came very slowly along the gorge as far as Dingur, a village of about thirty houses clustered together on the mountainside, and stopped here in the mosque.

The weather had now cleared after a storm of heavy rain and thunder the previous afternoon. We set off again at daybreak and passed Gulche, at the bottom of the gorge, a mile down the valley. After this we took the wrong track; we turned back to Gulche and marched from there down the other side of the river, through the gorge, to Kulatan. Some of the houses in this village were ornamented with markhor horns; others had their façades decorated with traditional carved patterns. We rested under some walnut trees by the river; then we marched on to Kotagal, a village similar to Kulatan but somewhat larger, and here we spent the night.

Beyond Kulatan we had to climb steeply to get along the track through the valley gorge. We stopped at a hamlet near the mouth of the Putut, a side-valley, where an elderly man gave us grapes. Then we waded across the river and followed the gorge along a high, narrow, shelving path to Saurel village, where a friendly old woman helped the porters as they carried their loads across a particularly nasty pitch of outward-sloping rock above a sheer drop.

All the way down the Minjigal valley we were plagued by minute black flies whose irritating bites caused us much discomfort.

We spent the night at Saurel. Next morning we descended from the gorge to a stretch of the valley known as Kotan. We marched along a stream bed, over some rough going, and then climbed 3,000 feet up a very steep mountainside covered with cedar and pine, to a pass leading into Nikrawal and, beyond that, to the Alingar valley.

We eventually got down to Nikra, an attractive village on the far side of the pass, before midday, and rested there in a walnut grove by the stream. From there a rough, difficult descent down the boulder-strewn hillside ended at Titi, where we camped, below the junction of the Nikrawal and Bizrakhail valleys.

The following morning, at dawn, we set off downstream. We passed along a continuous strip of cultivations, and three Nuristani villages which marked the end of my second journey in Nuristan. We now turned south-west, out of the Nikrawal valley, and climbed up an almost treeless, parched mountain-side, over another pass, into the valley of Alingar.

That night we camped in a Pathan village, under a sheltering vine, beside some rice-fields.

Here in the Alingar valley I paid off our five Safi porters and sent them back to their village in Pech. I then travelled on with Kemal ed Din and Ghulam Zubair to Jalalabad; and on 26 September we arrived once more in Kabul.

Ten days later, David Noel, military attaché at the British Embassy, drove me in his Land-Rover to Mazar-i-Sharif and Herat. Once again I saw the Kandaris, camped now in sheltered valleys, their black tents ranged along the river banks. We would stop the car for a moment, look, and then go on again. Fortunately the projected road on from Mazar-i-Sharif to Herat had as yet not been built. Each evening we camped beside the track, and I stayed awake and listened to the camel bells as the caravans made their way down this immemorial route. We passed Balkh, Mother of Cities, a grave-mound of the past, its monument a crumbling dome and ruined minarets, still of a beauty beyond belief. We visited the great mosque in Herat, its spacious court tranquil and impressive. I saw no other car in Herat. Then the bus arrived and I left for Meshed in Persia.

I would gladly have gone back another year to Mazar-i-Sharif and done that journey on foot, but the opportunity has passed. Now that the main road is built, the lorries thunder by; the camel caravans are gone, their bells stilled for ever.

EPILOGUE
LADAKH
1983

ON THESE JOURNEYS among the mountains of Kurdi-stan, Pakistan and Afghanistan, I had passed through some of the most spectacular country in the world and I had encountered people of many different races and origins, from Mongols to Nuristanis and Pathans. They varied greatly in their customs, the clothes they wore and in the lives they led; but all were Muslims, and this gave me a basic understanding of their behaviour. Though I had managed, in Peshawar and Kabul, to find someone who spoke English and was willing to accompany me, my inability to speak any of their languages kept me apart from my porters on these journeys and deprived me of the sense of comradeship I had known in Arabia and among the Madan in Iraq.

I went to India in 1983 and spent two months in Ladakh. For me this was a totally new experience, for here I was among Buddhists and with a people akin to the Tibetans.

Sir Robert ffolkes had been in Ladakh for the past five years, in charge of the Save the Children organization and he had invited me to join him there. He had advised me not to come before the beginning of September as the tourists would have left by then.

He met me in Srinagar on 4 September and a few days later he motored me by way of the Zoji-la Pass and Kargil, to Leh.

We set off from Leh on 17 September and for the next six weeks we travelled with ponies or yaks from one village to another. We crossed many passes, among them the Sisir-la, Kupa-la, and the 17,000-foot-high Sengyyi-la where a little snow still lingered. After descending from them in the bitter cold we sometimes arrived in a village after dark. Only in the Tibesti mountains in the Sahara had I seen a landscape as barren. We travelled incessantly over rocks and stones where the only vegetation was an occasional artemisia plant. Sometimes we crossed two passes a day, or skirted tremendous gorges. At last we would reach a small village with some cultivation along a stream, perhaps bordered by tamarisk and willow. Many of the villages had such strange, yet evocative names: Photoksar, Yulchung, Linkshet, Hanupata. Everywhere we were welcomed, for Robert ffolkes had done much to help these people. We would stay in a village for a day or two, and each night sit round a hearth in the increasing cold and drink their buttered tea. Some of these people, especially the old women, had striking faces. I was happy to be accepted by them, able to take what photographs I wanted with no feeling of restraint.

We returned briefly to Leh and visited the great monastery of Hemis; then we travelled through more of Ladakh's spectacular mountain valleys until in the last week of October we ended our journey back again once more near Leh, at the impressive Spituk monastery.

From Ladakh I went on to Jaipur, Pushkar and Jaisalmer in Rajasthan, Bandhavgarh in Bhopal, and Hyderabad; before returning to England from India the following year I spent a month in Nepal. I deliberately went to Nepal in March and April, being anxious to see the rhododendrons, but for some reason they were not in flower that year. I was aware that this was not a suitable time to see the Himalayas, which were then usually obscured by haze. I once caught a glimpse of the Annapurna range, clearcut and beautiful after a fall of rain. This was the vision I took away with me from the Himalayas, more than thirty years after I first travelled among the mountains.

INDEX